REASONING

WITH THE WORLD'S VARIOUS RELIGIONS

Examining and Evangelizing Other Faiths

EDWARD D. ANDREWS

REASONING

WITH THE WORLD'S VARIOUS RELIGIONS

Examining and Evangelizing Other Faiths

Edward D. Andrews

Christian Publishing House

Cambridge, Ohio

CPH
SINCE 2005

Christian Publishing House
Professional Christian Publishing of the Good News

REASONING WITH THE WORLD'S VARIOUS RELIGIONS: Examining and Evangelizing Other Faiths by Edward D. Andrews

ISBN-13: 978-1-945757-81-5

ISBN-10: 1-945757-81-7

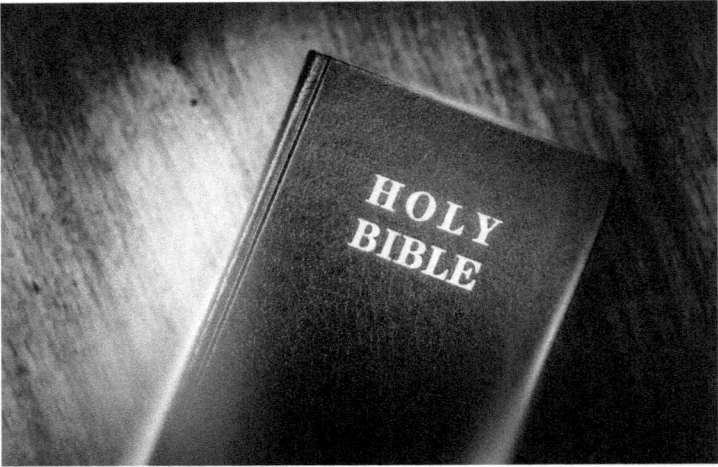

Table of Contents

INTRODUCTION to REASONING WITH THE WORLD'S VARIOUS RELIGIONS

1 Timothy 2:3-4 Updated American Standard Version (UASV)

³ This is good, and it is acceptable in the sight of God our Savior, ⁴ who desires all men to be saved and to come to an accurate knowledge[1] of truth.

Why Should We Be Interested in the Religion of Others?

The world has become a melting pot of people, cultures, and values, as well as many different religions. Religion has the greatest impact on the lives of mankind today. In India, Nepal, Bangladesh, Indonesia (especially in Bali- 84% Hindu), *Hinduism* is practiced, you will often see people doing puja, a prayer ritual performed by Hindus of devotional worship to one or more deities, or to host and honor a guest, or one to spiritually celebrate an event. Millions of Hindus flock each year to the river Ganges to be purified by its waters.

In Brazil, Mexico, the Philippines, the United States, and Italy *Catholic* are praying in churches and cathedrals while holding a crucifix or a rosary. The rosary refers to a form of prayer used in the Catholic Church and to the string of knots or beads used to count the component prayers that are offered in devotion to Mary. The nuns and priests are easily identified, as they are distinctive in their black garb.

In *Protestant* lands, chapels and churches abound, and on Sunday parishioners usually put on their best clothes and congregate to sing hymns and hear sermons. Often their clergy wear a black suit and a distinguishing clerical collar.

In Denmark, Estonia, Finland, the central, eastern and northern parts of Germany, Iceland, Latvia, Norway, Sweden, the United Kingdom, and the eastern, northern and western parts of Switzerland, as well as the United States, *Protestant* lands, you will find chapels and churches abound, and on Sunday churchgoers usually put on their best clothes and congregate to sing hymns and hear sermons, as well as a Bible study class. Many times, the minister, clergy, pastors, or elders are somewhat distinctive in that some wear black suits, or at least a suit while many churchgoers do not.

In Saudi Arabia, Yemen, Brunei, Qatar, Pakistan, United Arab Emirates, Iraq, Iran, Afghanistan, Sudan and Mauritania, *Islamic* countries, you can

---

[1] *Epignosis* is a strengthened or intensified form of *gnosis* (*epi*, meaning "additional"), meaning, "true," "real," "full," "complete" or "accurate," depending upon the context. Paul and Peter alone use *epignosis*.

hear the voices of men, the muezzins, who calls Muslims to prayer from the minaret of a mosque. These Muslim criers make the call from minarets five times each day, summoning the faithful to the *ṣalat*, that is, the ritual prayer of Muslims. All Muslims view the Holy Quran as the Islamic book of scripture. Under Islamic belief, the Quran was revealed by God and was given to the prophet Muhammad by the angel Gabriel in the seventh century C.E. the Islamic sacred book, believed to be the word of God as dictated to Muhammad by the archangel Gabriel and written down in Arabic. The Koran consists of 114 units of varying lengths, known as Surahs (a chapter or section of the Quran); the first Surah is said as part of the ritual prayer. These touch upon all aspects of human existence, including matters of doctrine, social organization, legislation, and holy war.

In Thailand, Myanmar, Bhutan, and Sri Lanka, we find the monks of *Buddhism*, usually in saffron, black, or red robes, who are viewed as a sign of piety. Ancient temples with the serene Buddha on display are evidence of the antiquity of the Buddhist faith, as some date to sixth century B.C.E.

In Japan, the *Shinto* religion is practiced in the daily life with family shrines and offerings being made to their ancestors. The Japanese pray for the most mundane things, even success in school examinations.

These are only a few of the major religions that make up billions of people throughout the earth. According to some estimates, there are roughly **4,200 religions** in the world. The word religion is sometimes used interchangeably with "faith" or "belief system", but religion differs from private belief in that it has a public aspect. What can we extrapolate from the variety of religions with billions of devoted adherents? Literally, for thousands of years mankind has tried to fill his spiritual needs. For thousands of years man has sought answer to the most troubling questions about life. Why is there so much suffering? Why are we here? How should we live? What are we actually? Why do we grow old, get sick, and eventually die? What does the future hold for mankind? Man has suffered with the trials and burdens of life, doubts about his future, and questions that seem to have no answer. Because man has an inherent spiritual need, religion, in many different ways, has sought to fill that need through God and gods, seeking the blessing from something greater than themselves.

Then again, there are millions of people around the world, who profess no religion nor any belief in a god (Atheism), or at least they cannot know for certain if there is some power (God) greater than themselves (Agnostics). However, that obviously does not mean that they are people without religion of principles or ethics, any more than professing a religion means that one does have them. One of the definitions of *religion* in the *Merriam-Webster Dictionary*, however, is this: "a cause, principle, or system of beliefs held to with ardor and faith." Certainly, atheism fits that

9

definition, and many atheists are quite zealous about their faith system, many being more zealous than much of Christianity. Another source, *The Shorter Oxford English Dictionary*, accepts religion as being "devotion to some principle; strict fidelity or faithfulness; conscientiousness; pious affection or attachment." Therefore, the atheist and the Agnostic have a religious devotion in their lives.

All disciples of Jesus Christ are to be Christian apologetic evangelists. (Matt. 24:14; 29-;19-20; Ac 1:8; 10:42; Jude 1:3, 22-23; 1 Pet. 3:15) If Christians are going to carry out the Great Commission, they need to know something about the background of the world's religions in order to be effective. Parrinder states in *World Religions—From Ancient History to the Present:* "To study different religions need not imply infidelity to one's own faith, but rather it may be enlarged by seeing how other people have sought for reality and have been enriched by their search." When we have at least a basic knowledge of other religions, this leads to understanding and understanding to tolerance of people with a different viewpoint, which is in no way suggesting that we accept anything unbiblical.

Why Examine Other Religions?

Many today see their religion as a very personal matter, which they are hesitant about discussing it with others. Largely the reason for this is because most are born into their religion because of where they were raised and the parents they had. Sadly, they are usually following the religion of their parents and grandparents with little or no idea about the religion itself. Therefore, religion for many is simply a family tradition. Thus, religion has been chosen for them.

In a sense, them, many in the world are assuming that their religion that they received at birth is the complete truth. If they were born in Italy or South America; then, without any choice on their part, they were likely raised a Catholic. On the other hand, if they were born in India, it is likely they were born into Hinduism or, if from the Punjab, perhaps a Sikh. Now, if their parents are from Pakistan, then there is little doubt that they were raised in Islam as a Muslim. Then, again, if they were raised in Russia, it is likely that they might be an atheist. –Galatians 1:13-14; Acts 23:6.

Therefore, it seems only wise that they ask if a religion that they were born into is automatically the true religion, which is approved by God. If the people of a thousand years ago had the mindset that the religion of my parents was good enough for them, it is good enough for me attitude, many among us would still be following practicing primitive shamanism and ancient fertility cults. It is at least enlightening and mind broadening for Christians to understand what others believe and how their beliefs originated. And it might also open up opportunities for Christian apologetic evangelists to share the truth of God's Word with them a sure hope for the future. Because of mass immigration over the past few decades, Christians are now sharing neighborhoods with people of many different religious backgrounds. Therefore, When the Christian evangelist understands their viewpoint, it can lead to more meaningful communication and conversation between two people of different faiths. Yes, it is true that there is a strong disagreement among many of the different religions, yet this is no reason for hating a person of a different faith or a different viewpoint. – 1 Peter 3:15; 1 John 4:20-21; Revelation 2:6.

The Mosaic Law stated, "You shall not take vengeance, nor bear any grudge against the sons of your people, but you shall love your neighbor as yourself; I am Jehovah." (Lev. 19:17-18) Jesus Christ stated, "But I say to you who hear, love your enemies, do good to those who hate you ... But love your enemies, and do good, and lend, expecting nothing in return, and your reward will be great, and you will be sons of the Most High, for he is kind to the ungrateful and the evil men." (Lu 6:27, 35) In evangelizing Islam, we can let the Muslim know that under the heading "She That Is To Be Examined," the Quran states a similar principle (surah 60:7, *MMP*): "It may be that Allah will bring about friendship between you and those of them whom you hold as enemies. And Allah is Powerful; and Allah is Forgiving, Merciful." How is it that we are to love our enemy? It means that we are willing to share the Gospel with them, a lifesaving message. While Christians are to be tolerant of others and open witnessing to persons from other religions, this does not mean that it makes no difference what one believes. They are not just different roads leading to the same place as some claim. It is the God of the Bible that is the determiner of what form of worship is acceptable. – Micah 6:8.

The Books of Moses, the first portion of the Holy Bible is the world's oldest religious book, which was initially penned under inspiration in the 16th and 15th centuries B.C.E. On the other hand, the Hindu writings of the Rig-Veda (a collection of hymns) were completed about 900 B.C.E. and do not claim divine inspiration. The Buddhist "Canon of the Three Baskets" dates back to the fifth century B.C.E. The Quran, claimed to have been transmitted from God through the angel Gabriel, was supposed given to Muhammad in the seventh century C.E. The Book of Mormon was allegedly given to Joseph Smith in the United States by an angel called Moroni in the 19th century. If any of these other so-called holy books were also divinely inspired, as is claimed by their adherents, they would not contradict the teachings of the Bible, which is the original inspired source.

REASONING 1 Introduction to Apologetics

Use of *REASONING FROM THE SCRIPTURES* should help you to cultivate the ability to reason from the Scriptures and to use them effectively in assisting others to learn about "the mighty works of God." – Acts 2:11.

Evangelism is the work of a Christian evangelist, of which all true Christians are obligated to partake to some extent, which seeks to persuade other people to become Christian, especially by sharing the basics of the Gospel, but also the deeper message of biblical truths. Today the Gospel is almost an unknown, so what does the Christian evangelist do? **Pre-evangelism** is laying a foundation for those who have no knowledge of the Gospel, giving them background information, so that they are able to grasp what they are hearing. The Christian evangelist is preparing their mind and heart so that they will be receptive to the biblical truths. In many ways, this is known as apologetics.

Christian apologetics [Greek: *apologia,* "verbal defense, speech in defense"] is a field of **Christian theology** which endeavors to offer a reasonable and sensible basis for the **Christian faith,** defending the faith against objections. It is reasoning from the Scriptures, explaining and proving, as one instructs in sound doctrine, many times having to overturn false reasoning before he can plant the seeds of truth. It can also be earnestly contending for the faith and saving one from losing their faith, as they have begun to doubt. Moreover, it can involve rebuking those who contradict the truth. It is being prepared to make a defense to anyone who asks the Christian evangelist for a reason for the hope that is in him or her. – Jude 1.3, 21-23; 1 Pet 3.15; Acts 17:2-3; Titus 1:9.

What do we mean by **obligated** and what we mean by **evangelism** are at the heart of the matter and are indeed related to each other?

EVANGELISM: An evangelist is a proclaimer of the gospel or good news, as well as all biblical truths. There are levels of evangelism, which is pictured in first-century Christianity. All Christians evangelized in the first century, but a select few fit the role of a full-time evangelist (Ephesians 4:8, 11-12), as was true of Philip and Timothy.

Both Philip and Timothy are specifically mentioned as evangelizers. (Ac 21:8; 2 Tim. 4:5) Philip was a full-time evangelist after Pentecost, who was sent to the city of Samaria, having great success. An angel even directed Philip to an Ethiopian Eunuch, to share the good news about Christ with him. Because of the Eunuch's already having knowledge of God by way of the Old Testament, Philip was able to help him understand that the Hebrew Scriptures pointed to Christ as the long-awaited Messiah. In the end, Philip baptized the Eunuch. After that, the Spirit again sent Philip on a mission, this time to Azotus and all the cities on the way to Caesarea. (Ac 8:5, 12, 14, 26-40) Paul evangelized in many lands, setting up one congregation after another. (2 Cor. 10:13-16) Timothy was an evangelizer or missionary, and Paul placed distinct importance on evangelizing when he gave his parting encouragement to Timothy. – 2 Timothy 4:5; 1 Timothy 1:3.

The office of apostle and evangelist seem to overlap in some areas but could be distinguished in that apostles traveled and set up congregations, which took evangelizing skills, but also developed the congregations after they were established. The evangelists were more of a missionary, being stationed in certain areas to grow and develop congregations. In addition, if we look at all of the apostles and the evangelists, plus Paul's more than one hundred traveling companions, it seems very unlikely that they could have had Christianity at over one million by the 125 C.E.[2] This was accomplished because all Christians were obligated to carry out some level of evangelism.

OBLIGATED: In the broadest sense of the term for evangelizer, all Christians are obligated to play some role as an evangelist.

• *Basic Evangelism* is planting seeds of truth and watering any seeds that have been planted. [In the basic sense of this word (euaggelistes), this would involve all Christians.] In some cases, it may be that one Christian planted the seed, which was initially rejected, so he was left in a good way because the planter did not try to force the truth down his throat. However, later he faces something in life that moves him to reconsider those seeds and another Christian water what had already been planted by the first Christian. This evangelism can be carried out in all of the methods that are available: informal, house-to-house, street, phone, internet, and the like. What amount of time is invested in the evangelism work is up to each Christian to decide for themselves?

• *Making Disciples* is having any role in the process of getting an unbeliever from his unbelief state to the point of accepting Christ as his Savior and being baptized. Once the unbeliever has become a believer, he is still developed until he has become strong. Any Christian could potentially carry this one person through all of the developmental stages. On the other hand, it may be that several have some part. It is like a person that specializes in a certain aspect of a job, but all are aware of the other aspects, in case they are called on to carry out that phase. Again, each Christian must decide for themselves what role they are to have, and how much of a role, but should be prepared to fill any role if needed.

---

[2] B.C.E. means "before the Common Era," which is more accurate than B.C. ("before Christ"). C.E. denotes "Common Era," often called A.D., for *anno Domini*, meaning "in the year of our Lord."

• *Part-Time or Full-Time Evangelist* is one who sees this as their calling and chooses to be very involved as an evangelist in their local church and community. They may work part-time to supplement their work as an evangelist. They may be married with children, but they realize their gift is in the field of evangelism. If it were the wife, the husband would work toward supporting her work as an evangelist and vice-versa. If it were a single person, he or she would supplement their work by being employed part-time, but also the church would help as well. This person is well trained in every aspect of bringing one to Christ.

• *Congregation Evangelists* should be very involved in evangelizing their communities and helping the church members play their role at the basic levels of evangelism. There is nothing to say that one church could not have many within, who take on part-time or full-time evangelism within the congregation, which would and should be cultivated.

Are You Prepared to Defend Your Christian Faith?

Have you ever been confronted by an unbeliever who had some challenging questions for you and you had to defend your Christian faith? Consider what happened to Julie, a 16-year-old Christian sister in Canada, who was in her ethics class. Her teacher made some very biblically incorrect comments about Christians. The teacher said, "Christianity is based on blind faith. Christianity is a laundry list of things to do and not do, meaning that Christians have no freedom or free will. Once you become a Christian, being saved by God's gift of grace, it does not matter what you do. The New Testament was written long after the events took place and are thus subject to legends being inserted into the text, as well as many mistakes, contradictions, and errors. The Bible has been changed or is otherwise not true to the original manuscripts. The Bible conflicts with science. The Bible promotes slavery. The Bible demeans women. The Bible is simply out of date, and should not be followed. The God of the Bible is immoral." How would you have reacted?

Julie prayed silently and then raised her hand. The class was almost over, and she knew that she could not address all those false statements about Christianity, the Bible, and God; so, she asked if should give a presentation about her the issues that the teacher had raised. The teacher readily agreed. Throughout the next two months, Julie prepared for the session, using the Bible study tools in her house and some online articles, and, of course, her study Bible.

The day of the presentation came, and Julie felt nervous but well prepared. She not only found rational, reasonable, and logical answers to the issues that were raised in class but also reasons given for the issues by unbelievers, Bible critics, and atheists. Anticipating these, she had ready responses to those as well, as she invited the class and the teacher to ask questions after her presentation. The ethics teacher was very impressed with Julie's Scriptural answers to the questions he had raised.

The question and answer discussion went on for 40 minutes. Then, Julie asked the class if they would like to watch the movie *The Case for Christ*;[3] where an investigative journalist, Lee Strobel, who was a self-proclaimed atheist that set out to disprove the existence of God after his wife became a Christian. All the students answered yes. So, the teacher scheduled another session the following day. After the video, Julie explained that many scientists, persons from many other highly educated fields had gone through similar life experiences. The teacher challenged her a little, saying, "yes, but just because some highly educated people accept something as true, this does not mean that it is true." Julie responded, "Yes, you are right, but it shows that the Christian faith, the Bible, and God are not just accepted by the lowly or uneducated as some people claim. Moreover, it isn't that these millions of educated people accept Christ, it is the reasons that they gave and have for accepting Christ that is your evidence."

Turning to Julie, the ethics teacher said, "You really do study the Bible and obviously make every effort to do what it says. For this alone, you deserve to be commended." The class applauded. The teacher went on to say, "Julie, you have persuaded me to take another look at the Bible and Christianity, a more objective one, where I will give the Christians a hearing ear this time." Julie explained that "not every Christian study the Bible as in-depth as they should, and many are unable to defend the faith, but this alone does not mean that the faith is not defendable."

Julie could have played it safe and remained silent. However, because she had a regular, consistent Bible study, seldom missed Christian meetings and found much joy in sharing her faith, she just could not hold herself back from witnessing about her Christian faith. This led to a teacher who was an ardent unbeliever rethinking his position and a class full of students, who now knew there was evidence to support the Bible as being authentic and true, that the idea of a Creator is not unreasonable, and Christianity deserves to be respected and heard. Julie took the initiative to defend her faith when the Bible, God, and Christianity was being challenged. Julie was obeying the Scriptural command, "sanctify Christ as Lord in your hearts, *always being prepared to make a defense*[4] to anyone who asks you for a

---

[3] http://www.imdb.com/title/tt6113488/
[4] Or *argument*; or *explanation*

reason for the hope that is in you; yet do it with gentleness and respect." –
1 Peter 3:15.

How Can I Defend My Belief in God?

The God of Judaism and Christianity has become a very unpopular topic these days for Christians living among unbelievers, the liberal media, and the liberal entertainment world. It is fine to mention almost anything else, sports, clothes, same-sex marriages, Islam, immigration, abortion, and you'll trigger a lively discussion. However, mention the God of the Bible, and an awkward silence may quickly descend. Many Christians today are almost embarrassed to discuss the Word of God, as they worry about what others might think of them. Many Christians will simply respond that religion is a personal matter that they do not talk about, even though they likely know that they are actually supposed to talk about the Bible but are commanded to do so for the purpose of converting the unbelievers. (Matt. 24:14; 28:19-20; Ac 1:8) What about you the reader? Are you nervous or reluctant to talk about God?

No one enjoys being rejected when trying to initiate discussions, and having the occasional person make sarcastic replies or even make fun of your belief in God is even worse! However, there are hundreds of millions of unbelievers out there with a receptive heart, and you might be surprised at their level of interest. Many of them are searching for answers to such deep questions as: Where is humanity heading? and Why is it so full of trouble? Many are curious about life after death.

Yes, today in this secular world, it is a daunting task to talk about the God of the Bible. Christians today are painted as the fanatical religion, even in the face of so much Islamic terrorism, they would rather talk to Muslims. It does boggle the rational mind how this can be so, but you need to come across as a fanatic, nor do you have to worry about saying exactly the right thing. Talking about your faith can be like learning something new. It is always challenging at first, but after a number of attempts it becomes easier, and your efforts will pay off. However, you might be thinking, "How do I get a conversation started in such a hostile environment?"

Usually, it is best to look for a comfortable moment. For instance, maybe there is a current event in the news that many are talking about, and you can offer some Scriptural insights. It is best to approach people one on one when it looks like they might have a few minutes to be engaged. Just know that many unbelievers have preconceived ideas about the Christian God, as well as the Bible itself. You have to be aware of these and have a ready response. This requires a little preparation on your part. Why don't we take a moment and defend the creation account?

If someone says to you, "in this modern, scientific world, is it reasonable to believe in creation?" How would you reply?

Almost always, evolution is presented as fact today, and the idea of a creator is presented as mere legend form an ancient outdated book. In that environment, it can be intimidating. How do you feel when the subject of evolution comes up? You believe that God "created all things." (Revelation 4:11) You see evidence of intelligent design all around you. However, the world of humankind alienated from God all believe life evolved from nothing. You might feel, "there are many textbooks today by reputable scientists, who am I to argue against them."

Rest assured, you are not by yourself in your feelings about the evolution theory. The fact is, even many scientists do not accept it. Neither do many professors and teachers, as well as many students. Still, if you are going to mount a defense in creation, you need to understand fully what the Bible really teaches on the subject. There is no need to argue points that Bible itself does not directly address. Let us look at a few examples.

All evolutionists will state the science has proven that the earth and our solar system have been in existence for billions of years. The bible says that the earth and our solar system was in existence prior to the first creative day, "In the beginning, God created the heavens and the earth." (Gen 1:1) As the Bible goes on to say, "And God began calling the light Day, and the darkness he called Night. And there came to be evening, and there came to be morning, the first day." (Gen. 1:5) Thus, it is clearly possible that the earth and the solar system has been in existence for billions of years, but human creation only thousands of years.

The evolutionist and the science textbooks will say that the earth could not have been created in six literal 24-hour creative days.[5] The Bible does not explicitly state that the creative days were literal 24-hour days but rather leans more in favor of six creative periods of unknown length.

Evolutionists and science textbooks will speak of several examples of changes in animals and humans that supposedly took place over millions of years. The Bible says, "'Let the waters swarm with swarms of living creatures, and let birds fly above the earth across the expanse of the heavens.' [21] So God went on to create[6] the great sea creatures and every living creature that moves, with which the waters swarm, according to their kinds, and every winged bird according to its kind. And God saw that it was good." (Gen. 1:20-21) The Bible does not support that life began from

---

[5] Genesis 1:1 BDC: Is the earth only 6,000 to 10,000 years old? Are the creative days literally, only 24 hours long?
http://tiny.cc/ru9cpy
[6] Progressive action indicated by the imperfect state

non-living matter or that God began the creation process of evolution with a single cell. Nevertheless, the Bible makes clear that each "kind" has the potential for great variety. Therefore, the Bible allows for micro-change to take place *within* each "kind."

We need to be confident in our beliefs. What level of evidence do you need to believe beyond a reasonable doubt in a Creator? Is the complexity of creation enough? Considering the enormous amount of evidence for creation, it's entirely reasonable to believe that we humans are the result of intelligent design. When the evidence is looked at objectively, it is really evolution that takes blind faith not creation. This is because the statistical odds for many evolutionary theories are millions of times beyond impossible, meaning evolution is miracles without the miracle maker. When you have bought out the time to reason this through, you will feel far more confident about being able to defend your faith, your belief in God the Creator, and his Word, the Bible.

REASONING   2 What is Christian Apologetics?

Can we use the Bible to defend the Christian faith, the Bible, and God Himself? Merely possessing faith is not sufficient. We must be prepared to defend it. It is vital that we be able to do so, for an apostle of Jesus Christ, Simon Peter, once wrote, "Sanctify Christ as Lord in your hearts, **always being prepared to make a defense** [Gr *apologia*] to anyone who asks you for a reason for the hope that is in you; yet do it with gentleness and respect." (1 Pet. 3:15) The word apologetics comes from the Greek term apologia, which is **"the act of making a defense."**[7] Yes, true Christians should be able to use the Bible to give a defense of their biblically grounded beliefs, the Word of God is inspired, fully inerrant, authoritative and the existence of God Himself. This requires serious investigation, asking questions, and obtaining answers from God's Word of truth the Bible, as well as biblical archaeology, original language manuscripts, history, and many other areas of study.

In proclaiming and defending the good news and when called upon to give a reason for our hope, we should always be prepared as much as possible to give an answer, or at best go do research if we do not have a ready answer for anyone with a receptive heart. Daily personal Bible study will be a requirement if we want to be a productive Christian evangelist. You must thoroughly know what you want to defend against all kinds of unbelievers. Therefore, buy out time to study God's Word. Do not think that we are too young or too old. Do not think that our secular education is not good enough. Whether we are young or old, having a college or university education or lower education, we can all learn to know our Bible. Use the Bible daily in conversation; as well as daily personal study and reading and meditation, even if it is only for fifteen, thirty, or sixty minutes, then we will surely become a real artist in the use of God's Word regardless of our age and education. What we do consistently and regular daily we will eventually master. Daily personal Bible study is one of the most important aspects of our Christian walk with God in developing the ability to preach and defend the true faith and hope effectively. Christians must learn the Word of God well. The Apostle Paul told Titus, "Our people must also learn to engage in good works to meet necessary needs so that they will not be unfruitful." (Titus 3:14) Through Bible study, we prepare ourselves so that our "speech [is] always ... gracious, seasoned with salt, so

---

[7] William Arndt et al., *A Greek-English Lexicon of the New Testament and Other Early Christian Literature* (Chicago: University of Chicago Press, 2000), 117.

that [we] may know how [we] ought to answer each person." – Colossians 4:6.

The Greek Term Apologia

Apologetics: (Gr. *apologia*) The term literally means "to defend" and is used in the biblical sense to refer to ones who defend the Christian faith, the Bible, and God in speech or in written form. The Christian apologist attempts to prove that the Christian faith, the Bible, and God are reasonable, logical, necessary and right. – Ac 25:16; 2 Cor. 7:11; Phil. 1:7, 16; 2 Tim. 4:16; 1 Pet. 3:15

Two Kinds of Apologetics

There are two basic kinds of apologetics. There is negative apologetics and positive apologetics.

Negative Apologetics

In negative apologetics, the Christian apologist is playing defense. We can use sports as an analogy. Whether it be baseball, football, or basketball, when we are playing defense, we cannot score any points. The only task we have while playing defense is to prevent the other team from scoring any points. Therefore, the atheist, agnostic, or Bible critic that has some kind of problem with the Christian faith, the Bible, or God raises issues that they believe undermine the Christian beliefs. They are on the offense, trying to score points. In playing defense, the Christian apologist only needs to show that this objection that was raised is not valid, it is unreasonable, illogical. There is no real substance to it. In this scenario, the burden of proof is on the unbeliever who is raising the issues. Negative apologetics is always easier than positive apologetics.

Burden of Proof

The Burden of Proof: The burden of proof in a criminal trial is on the prosecution. The defense attorney only needs to undermine the argument(s) for guilt by the prosecution are not valid. The burden of proof in a trial of the Christian faith is on the unbeliever bringing the case. Either their arguments are valid, or they are not. The Christian apologist need not prove his innocence so to speak, just that the case against him has no merit. The burden of proof falls on the one making the claims. If the Christian is witnessing to another, he has the burden to prove what he says is so if asked for proof. However, if the critic is challenging the Christian, the burden of disproving lies with the critic. The closer the claim is to socially accepted knowledge, less proof is needed, while the further one moves from conventional knowledge, the more evidence is required. I believe that the legal burden of proof offers the best answers to the witnessing of others.

It has been refined over the last 200 years to the point of evaluating a life that is held in its balance, just as everlasting life is held in the balance. Below we will list the levels of legal proof and some percentage and wording to indicate the degree of certainty needed. We have used different Bible objects for each one, but any criticism could be plugged into that particular burden of proof.

Problem of Evil

Without a doubt, the *problem of evil* is the most difficult Bible difficulty that Christians have to answer. The problem of evil refers to the question of how to reconcile the existence of wickedness and suffering when there is an all knowing, all powerful, loving God. The problem of evil is so serious that we can say, if a Christian is going to have doubts, this is the only issue it should take place because all other Bible difficulties are easily resolved in comparison. Under the burden of proof, the unbeliever who brings up the problem of evil is responsible for showing that this is a sufficient enough reason for not believing in God. The Christian apologist only needs to show that that the problem of evil is not sufficient enough for not believing in God and need not provide an answer to the issue. Nevertheless, in APOLOGIST 3, we answer the problem of evil. We just need to show that there is a morally sufficient reason for God temporarily allowing evil to exist.

Positive Apologetics

Returning to our sports analogy, here in positive apologetics, the Christian is now playing offense, trying to score points, while the unbeliever is on defense, trying to prevent us from scoring points. Under positive apologetics, the Christian now has to own the fact that he or she is under the burden of proof. In other words, we are offering arguments, information, explanations, or evidence that will help the receptive person to accept biblical truths, with the eventuality of their accepting the Christian faith. We are trying to prove the existence of God, as well as that the Bible is the inspired, fully inerrant Word of God and that it is authentic and true. The unbeliever is trying to show that our arguments are not the valid or not that effective.

Legal Terms as to How We Should Objectively View Bible Evidence

There are approximately 3,000+ of these supposed errors and contradictions in the Bible. It would take us several volumes to consider such an undertaking. Please do not be disheartened by such a large number, because there are compelling reasons why we have so many Bible difficulties, not errors or contradictions. If we offer reasonable responses and satisfactory answers for these challenging passages, it can be inferred that there would be a rational answer for the few that may not have a reply as of yet as well.

One reason for having this new way of looking at evidence is the new atheist. The unbeliever of decades past was satisfied to believe that everything came about by chance, through evolution, and not concern himself with what others believed. This is no longer the case. Sadly, today's atheist is more involved in leading the Christian down the path of doubt, while the Christian denominations are almost entirely inactive in evangelizing the unbeliever. Hundreds of atheistic books and videos are flooding the market in an attempt to discredit the Bible, the foundation of the Christian belief system. Another enemy of God's Word is found in the agnostic. An agnostic teaches that it is hard to know whether God exists and that we are unable to accept the Bible as a revelation of that existence. Below we better define how we should view available evidence.

Burden of Proof: The burden of proof falls on the one making the claims. If the Christian is witnessing to another, he has the burden to prove what he says is so if asked for proof. However, if the critic is challenging the Christian, the burden of disproving lies with the critic. The closer the claim is to socially accepted knowledge, less proof is needed, while the further one moves from conventional knowledge, the more evidence is required. I believe that the legal burden of proof offers the best answers to the witnessing of others. It has been refined over the last 200 years to the point of evaluating a life that is held in its balance, just as everlasting life is held in the balance. Below we will list the levels of legal proof and some percentage and wording to indicate the degree of certainty needed. We have used different Bible objects for each one, but any criticism could be plugged into that particular burden of proof.

Warrants Further Investigation

Reasonable (30%): This is a low-level burden of proof in that it is enough to accept something as *reasonably likely*, being so unless proven otherwise by a deeper look, which may bring in more evidence. For example, at this level, it is reasonably likely that Jesus Christ lived, died and was resurrected. This may be achieved in the first conversation with the one with which we are sharing the good news.

Probable (40%): This is also a low-level burden of proof in that it is enough to accept something as *likely being so* unless proven otherwise by a deeper look, which may bring in more evidence. At this level, it is probable that the Bible is the inspired, inerrant Word of God. This may be achieved in the first 2-3 conversations with the one with which we are sharing the good news.

Conviction for Claim

Preponderance of Evidence (51%): This is a higher-level burden of proof that makes Noah surviving a worldwide flood *more likely to be true than not true*.

Clear and Convincing Evidence (85%): This is an even higher level of burden of proof that Adam and Eve were historical persons, created by God is substantially *far more likely than not*.

Beyond Reasonable Doubt (99%): This is the highest level of burden of proof that over forty major prophecies about Jesus Christ in the Old Testament came true, being beyond reasonable doubt. It must be understood that feeling as though we *have no reason to doubt* is not the same as 100 percent absolute evidence of certainty. If one has doubts that affect their belief of certainty, it is not beyond reasonable doubt. This too must be qualified, because it is reasonable **to have doubts about certain aspects of the whole** that does not have all the answers as of yet, but it **does not affect the level of certainty as a whole.**

Evidentialism (a theory of justification according to which the justification of a belief depends solely on the evidence for it) only becomes self-defeating the moment one tries to raise the level of certainty to the absolute instead of beyond reasonable doubt (*sufficient evidence*). The argument against the use of evidentialism that the principle simply does not account for the way we come to have most of our beliefs is no real argument at all. A belief that cold weather makes you sick is not the same as believing there is an Almighty God, Creator. Each of us has hundreds of thousands of core beliefs that are accepted as fact until we come across something that tells us otherwise. Ironically, we are told to investigate before buying a car, or especially a house, as it is a big commitment. Yet, are we to equate the acceptance and commitment to Christ the same way we do that a chair will hold our weight, or our car will get us to work?

The Bible critic generally exaggerates the level of his evidence, presenting it in a sly fashion. At the same time, he will arbitrarily dismiss the Christian evidence, by declaring that all who believes in God and the Bible are foolish and naive. The simple principle to be observed here is to ask, 'which is more likely to be true based on what you know.' Of course, as one grows in knowledge, one's belief is subject to change, i.e., it is either strengthened (reinforced), or it is cast aside. A Christian that falls away due to atheism or agnosticism (like Dr. Bart D. Ehrman) will after that require absolute evidence rather than evidence beyond a reasonable doubt. From that time on, God must then show him all that his doubting heart desires. The common expression being, "God if you just _____, I will believe."

The Bible critic runs around like a scavenger looking for an error, not reason. As they come upon a pebble of doubt, they throw it out as though it were a boulder of truth against God. Six months later, an archaeologist digging in Bible lands somewhere finds something that utterly and entirely removes this critic's evidence. Does the critic even lean a little closer to God? No, because Christian evidence, no matter how weighty, does not exist on the critic's agenda, which is to sow seeds of doubt regarding the Bible's authenticity. Even if the Ark of the Covenant with the Ten Commandments and Aaron's rod that budded were to be located, the critic would still maintain their stand because the unearthing of these objects does not meet their agenda.

For example, the Bible critic will argue from silence, saying 'Belshazzar of the Bible has not been found in secular history, we have no evidence that he ever existed.' Now, say a year later, a piece of a tablet is found that mentions Belshazzar (this has actually happened), and in connection with the historical account in the Bible. Well, that critic does not draw closer to where the evidence is pointing; he throws it out, dismissing it as though he never raised the argument, and runs to look for another. This same Bible critic then argues that Shalmaneser never existed, 'there is no evidence to support his existence,' he says. A short time later, archaeological evidence comes to light that supports Shalmaneser's existence. Yet, this critic is off to his next claim without even a hint of doubting his doubt. Sadly, this circle of madness just keeps going.

THE ATHEIST: Mistaken Views of Christianity, the Bible, and God

Atheists make some valid points about the difficulty that Christians and Christianity find themselves in today. However, it is more complex than what they believe to be true. The reason atheism is booming (if we could even use that term with such a small amount), is because of biblical illiteracy within Christianity. Christianity is 90% biblically illiterate. These ones are barely able to explain their doctrinal positions let alone defend the faith. Moreover, atheists are more apologetic and evangelistic about their beliefs. In addition, atheists tend to read more atheistic apologetic books that supposedly undermine Christianity, the Bible, and God. Christians are just now finding their way into Christian apologetics.

The last 40-50 years have seen many Christian leaders taking on Christian apologetics and Christian Philosophy being of serious interest. The irony is, if an atheist, who is well read comes across dozens of biblically illiterate Christians online, they believe that Christianity, the Bible, and God are indefensible. However, this is not the case because if they were to encounter a William Lane Craig, Norm Geisler, Ravi Zacharias, John

Lennox, Gary Habermas, Hugh Ross, or any one of the hundreds of other Christian apologists, it would be a completely different outcome.

What many fail to understand is, Christianity being attacked by the so-called intellectuals of the world is nothing new, it has gone on for 2,000 years. Think about this, in 33 C.E.[8] there were 120 Christians in a world of Greek Philosophy. Within 120 years, the number of Christians grew to over a million out of a one hundred million population. However, this was also the era that began the fragmentation of Christianity too. Will Durant states: "Celsus [second-century opponent of Christianity] himself had sarcastically observed that Christians were 'split up into ever so many factions, each individual desiring to have his own party.' About 187 [C.E.] Irenaeus listed twenty varieties of Christianity; about 384 [C.E.] Epiphanius counted eighty."—The Story of Civilization: Part III—Caesar and Christ.

Today there are over 41,000 different varieties of Christianity, all divided against one another, all believing different from one another, all being vastly biblically illiterate. One might think this only spells the demise of Christianity. However, Jesus and the other New Testament authors all spoke of the great apostasy that was coming, which would fragment the Christian faith founded by Christ and grown by the apostles. They spoke of true Christianity and false Christianity, and that both would grow together but that false Christianity would outgrow true Christianity. This has come true exactly as it was described in great detail 2,000 years ago. On the horizon is a great harvest that is to come where there will be a reckoning for those Christians who believed that they were doing the right thing but like the atheist and agnostic, they are very much mistaken.

Matthew 7:21-23 Updated American Standard Version (UASV)

[21] **"Not everyone** [i.e., not every Christian] who says to me, 'Lord, Lord,' will enter the kingdom of heaven, but **the one who does the will of my Father** who is in heaven. [22] On that day **many will say** to me, 'Lord, Lord, did we not prophesy in your name, and cast out demons in your name, and do many mighty works in your name?' [23] And then **I will declare to them,** 'I never knew you; depart from me, you who practice lawlessness.'

- Not every Christian will be found to have a righteous standing before God at Jesus second coming

- Only those doing the will of the Father will have a righteous standing

---

[8] B.C.E. means "before the Common Era," which is more accurate than B.C. ("before Christ"). C.E. denotes "Common Era," often called A.D., for *anno Domini,* meaning "in the year of our Lord."

- Thus, the question that begs to be answered is, "what is the will of the Father according to God's Word not our subjective opinion?"

- The vast majority of Christians and Christianity believe that they are the truth and the way today and that they are doing the will of the Father

- However, to these ones, Jesus will say, 'I never knew you; depart from me, you who practice lawlessness.'

There is the mistaken view that true Christians want to save the whole of humankind. This is not true; they are not interested in those unbelievers with unreceptive hearts. They are not interested in those unbelievers with closed minds. They are not interested in false Christians who are blinded by their theological biases. The evangelistic objective is that true Christians save some but that they evangelize all. Right now, true Christianity is getting its footing back and is growing defenders of the faith. THE CULTURE WAR: How the West Lost Its Greatness & Was Weakened From Within by Hanne Nabintu Herland is a part of that wakeup call. Christian Publishing House and thousands of Christian apologists around the world are building an army of Christian defenders of the faith, of God's Word, and of God Himself.

REASONING 3 What Will You Say to a Jehovah's Witness?

"You will be my witnesses ... to the End of the Earth." – ACTS 1:8.

Not All Christian Apologetic Arguments Are Equal

We will use some arguments often raised about Jehovah's Witnesses as our text case. J. Warner Wallace is a leading Evangelical Christian apologist today. On his blog, he has the article titles, "10 Important Questions for the Jehovah's Witness Worldview." Therein he writes,

One way to examine the Jehovah's Witness perspective is simply to see how well it answers a few important philosophical and theological questions as we examine what the Jehovah's Witness religion teaches. The following questions are designed to challenge the Jehovah's Witness claims about reality and help you to initiate a discussion with your friends or family who may hold this worldview:

Philosophical Questions

Let's begin with some questions springing from basic philosophical concerns:

A primary concern in asking questions that undermine another's faith is never to ask any question that also applies to your side of the fence as well. Before we look at the 10 questions, let us consider some basics.

The Greek Term Apologia

Apologetics: (Gr. *apologia*) The term literally means "to defend" and is used in the biblical sense to refer to ones who defend the Christian faith, the Bible, and God in speech or in written form. The Christian apologist attempts to prove that the Christian faith, the Bible, and God are reasonable, logical, necessary and right. – Ac 25:16; 2 Cor. 7:11; Phil. 1:7, 16; 2 Tim. 4:16; 1 Pet. 3:15

Books to Help You Explain Your Belief

- REVIEWING 2013 New World Translation of Jehovah's Witnesses: Examining the History of the Watchtower Translation and the Latest Revision

- INVESTIGATING JEHOVAH?S WITNESSES: Why 1914 Is Important to Jehovah's Witnesses

Two Kinds of Apologetics

There are two basic kinds of apologetics. There is negative apologetics and positive apologetics.

Negative Apologetics

1914 THE FALL WATCHTOWER PROPHECY

INVESTIGATING
JEHOVAH'S WITNESSES
WHY 1914 IS IMPORTANT TO JEHOVAH'S WITNESSES
EDWARD D. ANDREWS

In negative apologetics, the Christian apologist is playing defense. We can use sports as an analogy. Whether it be baseball, football, or basketball, when we are playing defense, we cannot score any points. The only task we have while playing defense is to prevent the other team from scoring any points. Therefore, the atheist, agnostic, or Bible critic that has some kind of problem with the Christian faith, the Bible, or God raises issues that they believe undermine the Christian beliefs. They are on the offense, trying to score points. In playing defense, the Christian apologist only needs to show that this objection that was raised is not valid, it is unreasonable, illogical. There is no real substance to it. In this scenario, the burden of proof is on the unbeliever who is raising the issues. Negative apologetics is always easier than positive apologetics.

Burden of Proof

The burden of Proof: The burden of proof in a criminal trial is on the prosecution. The defense attorney only needs to undermine the argument(s) for guilt by the prosecution are not valid. The burden of proof in a trial of the Christian faith is on the unbeliever bringing the case. Either their arguments are valid, or they are not. The Christian apologist need not prove his innocence so to speak, just that the case against him has no merit. The burden of proof falls on the one making the claims. If the Christian is witnessing to another, he has the burden to prove what he says is so if asked for proof. However, if the critic is challenging the Christian, the burden of disproving lies with the critic. The closer the claim is to socially accepted knowledge, less proof is needed, while the further one moves from conventional knowledge, the more evidence is required. I believe that the legal burden of proof offers the best answers to the witnessing of others. It has been refined over the last 200 years to the point of evaluating a life that is held in its balance, just as everlasting life is held in the balance. Below we will list the levels of legal proof and some percentage and wording to indicate the degree of certainty needed. We have used different Bible objects for each one, but any criticism could be plugged into that particular burden of proof.

Problem of Evil

Without a doubt, the *problem of evil* is the most difficult Bible difficulty in answering. The problem of evil refers to the question of how to reconcile the existence of wickedness and suffering when there is an all knowing, all powerful, loving God. The problem of evil is so serious that we can say, if a Christian is going to have doubts, this is the only issue it should take place because all other Bible difficulties are easily resolved in comparison. Under the burden of proof, the unbeliever who brings up the problem of evil is responsible for showing that this is a sufficient enough reason for not believing in God. The Christian apologist only needs to show that that the problem of evil is not sufficient enough for not believing in God and need not provide an answer to the issue. Nevertheless, in APOLOGIST 3, we answer the problem of evil. We just need to show that there is a morally sufficient reason for God temporarily allowing evil to exist.

Positive Apologetics

Returning to our sports analogy, here in positive apologetics, the Christian is now playing offense, trying to score points, while the unbeliever is on defense, trying to prevent us from scoring points. Under positive apologetics, the Christian now has to own the fact that he or she is under the burden of proof. In other words, we are offering arguments, information, explanations, or evidence that will help the receptive person to accept biblical truths, with the eventuality of their accepting the Christian faith. We are trying to prove the existence of God, as well as that the Bible is the inspired, fully inerrant Word of God and that it is authentic and true. The unbeliever is trying to show that our arguments are not the valid or not that effective.

We must understand that not all Christian apologetic augments are equal. Some arguments have liabilities when they are used. Now, understand, this author has written a book undermining the beliefs of the

Jehovah's Witnesses, so this exercise below is only to demonstrate that some Christian apologetic questions are not effective and will backfire.

Wallace's 10 Questions

If I am to accept the teaching of the Jehovah's Witness religion, I am first going to have to trust the source of this teaching. But how can I trust someone who claims to speak for God when they have been wrong about prior predictions?

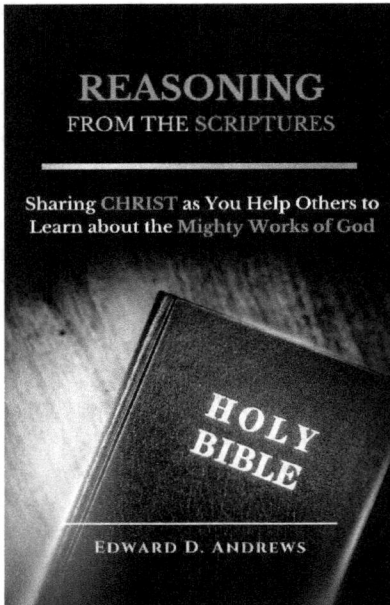

REASONING
FROM THE SCRIPTURES

Sharing CHRIST as You Help Others to
Learn about the Mighty Works of God

HOLY
BIBLE

EDWARD D. ANDREWS

RESPONSE: The Witnesses will only say that under your logic, we would also reject Protestantism and all of their 41,0000 denominations because many Protestant leaders have predicted dates and were clearly wrong **(William Miller** (February 15, 1782 – December 20, 1849) was an American Baptist). They would also point out that the founding fathers of major Christian denominations of today, committed atrocious acts in their history, such as killing or having killed other Christians who dared to believe differently. During the Reformation the Calvinists had many arrested, tried, and executed by slow burning for daring to believe differently. Calvin justified his actions in these atrocities by saying, "When the papists are so harsh and violent in defense of their superstitions that they rage cruelly to shed innocent blood, are not Christian magistrates shamed to show themselves less ardent in defense of the sure truth?" Will Durant, THE REFORMATION: A History of European Civilization from Wyclif to Calvin, 1300-1564 (The Story of Civilization)(New York City: Simon & Schuster, 1980), 482.

Jehovah's Witnesses claim to be the only religious organization speaking for God but don't the Roman Catholic, and Mormon religions make very similar claims? Why should I trust the Jehovah's Witnesses?

RESPONSE: The Witnesses will only say that all Christian denominations believe that they are the truth and the way. There are 41,000 different denominations, all believing different from the others, even to the point of contradiction. Certainly, they cannot all be right. This includes the so-called salvation doctrines as well.

The divisiveness would never work in an effort to fulfill the great commission of making disciples. What if we just singled out the Baptist church as our test case. There are over well 50,000 Baptist churches in the United States. There are literally 61 different Baptist divisions, i.e., subdivision denominations within the Baptist Church. Yes, they all believe differently as well. What if we just select one of this subdivision denominations, will we finally find a oneness of mind and teachings? No. Why? There exists yet another divisive problem, in that the Baptist churches as a whole are autonomous, which means that every individual church has the freedom to act independently and teach differently than the others. The irony is, they will argue that they are in agreement when it comes to the so-called salvation doctrines. Yet, this is not true because every one of the so-called salvation doctrines has anywhere from two to four different positions or views.

DIVERSITY OF BIBLICAL INTERPRETATION
DIVERSITY OF CHRISTIAN BELIEFS

In his forward to R. C. Sproul's Knowing Scripture, J. I. Packer observes that Protestant theologians are in conflict about biblical interpretation. To illustrate the diversity of biblical interpretations, William Yarchin pictures a shelf full of religious books saying different things, but all claiming to be faithful interpretations of the Bible. Bernard Ramm observed that such diverse interpretations underlie the "doctrinal variations in Christendom." A mid-19th century book on biblical interpretation observed that even those who believe the Bible to be "the word of God" hold "the most discordant views" about fundamental doctrines." Below are just a few examples.

Four Views of Hell	Four Views of Salvation	Two Views of Inspiration	Three Views of Atonement
Four Views of creation	Four Views of Eternal Security	Four Views of Inspiration	Four Views of Works in Final Judgment
Four Views of Inerrancy	Four Views of Sanctification	Two Views of Fasting	Four Views of the Book of Revelation
Two Views of Christology	Three Views of Image of God	Three Views of Grace	Three Views of Human Constitution
Four Views of Providence	Two Views of Lord's Supper	Four Views of Free Will	Two Views of Charismatic Gifts
Two Views of Baptism	Three Views of Jesus' Return	Two Views of Sabbath	Four Views of Predestination
Three Views of Purgatory	Four Views of the Church	Four Views of End Times	Four Views of Christian Spirituality
Four Views of Antichrist	Three Views of Neutrality	Three Views of Heaven	Two Views of Foreknowledge

Zanesville, Ohio has eleven Baptist churches, in a community of 150,000 people. What if all eleven Baptist churches decided independently that they were going to go out and evangelize the community to make disciples? How could that even work? Suppose an unbeliever is visited by several different subdivision Baptist denominations and is told different views about the same doctrine? How is the unbeliever going to take Christianity seriously with such division as this? Moreover, we have other problems that we have not even addressed.

Press on to Maturity

Hebrews 5:13-6:1 Updated American Standard Version (UASV)

[13] For everyone who partakes of milk is unacquainted with the word of righteousness, for he is an infant. [14] But solid food belongs to the mature,

to those who through practice have their discernment trained to distinguish between good and evil. **6** Therefore, leaving behind the elementary doctrine about the Christ, let us press on to maturity, not laying again a foundation of repentance from dead works and faith in God,

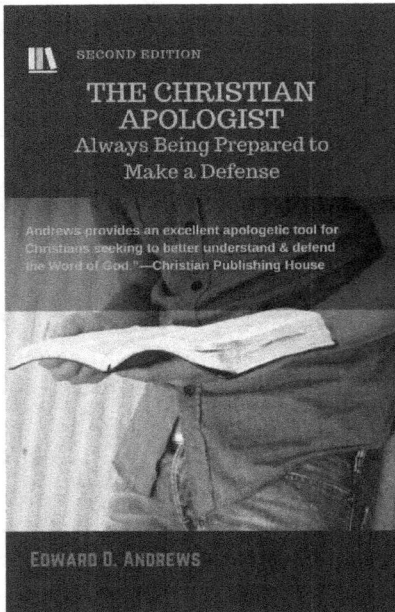

The problem of biblical illiteracy is well known but truly ignored. 90% of Christians are biblically illiterate in that they cannot explain the foundational doctrines of the faith or defend the Word of God as inspired, fully inerrant, and authoritative. Yes, they know some cute Bible stories and some Bible principles. This problem has existed for over a hundred years, and nothing has truly been done to address it. Then, we couple biblical illiteracy with the fact that **almost no Christians are being trained** to make disciples in their churches. Thus, we have 41,000 different denominations all teaching differently. We have tens of thousands of churches in the same denomination broken off into different sub-divisional denominations, and even a single subdivision has autonomous churches that believe differently, and the individual church has members that believe differently, with 90% being biblically illiterate and having no evangelism training. How do we fix that atrocious problem, so as to carry out the Great Commission? J. Warner Wallace continues,

The Jehovah's Witness translation of the Bible condemns false prophecy and says unfulfilled prophecy is an indicator God is not speaking through that Prophet and we should not, therefore, pay attention to what that prophet is saying. So shouldn't this also apply to the teaching of the Watchtower?

RESPONSE: The Witnesses will only say this question is similar to the first one above. There have been many Protestant church leaders set false dates, predict false things. Thus, this argument like the other will only cause a self-inflicted wound.

Jehovah's Witnesses often talk about John 1:1 and argue the original Greek wording is more correctly translated "In the beginning was the Word, and the Word was with God, and the Word was ¬a god", rather than the orthodox rendering, "In the beginning was the Word, and the

Word was with God, and the Word was God." But if this is true why do so many translators agree with the orthodox view?

RESPONSE: The Witnesses will only say I am not going to argue the Greek grammar because the Witnesses reason for translating John 1:1 as such is by following the Protestant religions grammar books, which all do not agree by the way. What I will point out Mr. Wallace is your last point. You asked, "*if this is true why do so many translators agree with the orthodox view?*" The majority of something does not in and of itself make something correct; otherwise, we would all be Catholic or Muslim.

Jehovah's Witnesses often argue God's true name is "Jehovah". But if this is true, why doesn't the word, "Jehovah" appears in the New Testament?

RESPONSE: Wallace, Jehovah was used by Bible scholars up unto the 20th century. Look at the names in your Bible. Many Hebrew kings and others used by God personally in Bible times used part of the Father's personal name in their name, like **Jeho**ash, **Jeho**ram, Jehoiakim, Jehoiachin, **Jeho**ram, **Jeho**hanan, **Jeho**nadab, Jehoahaz, and even the wife of High Priest Jehoiada; daughter of King **Jeho**ram of Judah, **Jeho**sheba, among many more. We notice that the beginning of the Father's personal name is used in every one of these cases. Does anyone find it a bit troubling that the Bibles (JB, LEB, HCSB), which choose to use the so-called scholarly "Yahweh" rendering still spell the above names with Jeho? Why do these same translations not spell Jehoash "Yahash"? Moreover, the 1901 American Standard Version uses Jehovah. Lastly, we do not have the original New Testament manuscripts, so we cannot say with certainty that the name Jehovah was not in there.

Jehovah's Witnesses say 144,000 people will be part of the "anointed Class' who will live with God in Heaven and will reign over the 'Great Crowd'. But doesn't the Bible describe this group in contradiction to what Jehovah's Witnesses believe?

RESPONSE: All I can say here is the Bible makes it clear that not all good people are going to heaven. If the Witnesses are false over this misinterpretation, all Protestant religions have misinterpreted the Bible since the Reformation. The renowned Robert L. Thomas, Jr., professor of New Testament at The Master's Seminary in the United States, wrote, "The case for symbolism is exegetically weak." He added: "It is a definite number [at 7:4] in contrast with the indefinite number of 7:9. If it is taken symbolically, no number in the book can be taken literally." —*Revelation: An Exegetical Commentary,* Volume 1, page 474.

Why Do Jehovah's Witnesses feel the need to make obvious changes to certain passages of Scripture?

RESPONSE: Your reference to the square brackets in the 1984 edition of the New World Translation is a mistaken notion. The square brackets [ ] enclose words inserted to complete the sense in the English text. This is done by all translations and in some these words are italicized. Moreover, again, it is your grammars that advocate for some of these additions. More importantly, you might be better focusing on the more than 50 dynamic equivalent translations where so-called true Christians have produced interpretive translations instead of the literal Word of God. CHOOSING YOUR BIBLE: Bible Translation Differences

Jehovah's Witnesses obviously deny Jesus is God, but how can they do this when Scripture repeatedly describes Jesus as Divine?

RESPONSE: Divine does not equal God. The Greek terms simply mean a divine person.

How Can Jehovah's Witnesses claim Jesus was a created being when Jesus created everything ever created?

RESPONSE: Jesus was the first divine person to be created and then he became the master worker of the Father and created all things.

1 Corinthians 15:27-28 Updated American Standard Version (UASV)

[27] For he [the Father] put all things in subjection under his [Jesus'] feet. But when he says, "All things are put in subjection," it is evident that he [God the Father] is excepted who put all things in subjection to him. [28] When all things are subjected to him [Jesus, the Son], then the Son himself also will be subjected to the One who subjected all things to him, so that God may be all in all.

If you are going to ask an apologetic question to undermine a belief or a translation be certain that your side is also not guilty of the same things or it is not your grammars that they depend on for their translation renderings.

Witnessing to the Jehovah's Witnesses

Yes, Jehovah's Witnesses are mistaken in a number of biblical doctrines but not on everything they teach. Moreover, so-called true Christians have also been mistaken on many Bible doctrines as well and over time with a better understanding; they arrived at the correct teaching. When you over exaggerate by calling the Jehovah's Witnesses a cult you only give them more fuel in their evangelism work because they will define a cult and show examples of real cults (Jim Jones, Charles Manson, David Koresh). This only makes it easier for the Witnesses to pull Christians away from the so-called true Christianity. In addition, many of the doctrinal positions that the

34

Witnesses hold are actually borrowed from other denominations of Christendom within the last 2,000 years. The Christian evangelist needs to win Witnesses back into the fold of true Christianity, as well as protect the sheep currently within the fold. We do not do that by over exaggerating our evidence or forgetting that our denominations taught similarly or that Protestant church leaders have made similar mistakes or trying to demean a religion by name calling when they do not even fit the definition or characteristics of a cult.

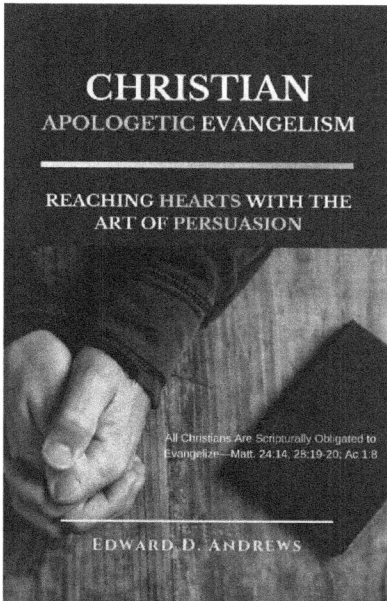

The fact that I even uttered the above truths about the Witnesses will drive some to believe I am an apologist for the Witnesses. Some readers will feel completely uncomfortable even uttering positive things about the Witnesses or admitting that Protestant denominations have made similar mistakes, some much worse. What does this sound like? It sounds like some so-called true Christian leaders have carried out a little mind control themselves. Most Christian leaders attempt to label the Jehovah's Witness, the Mormons, and the Seventh Day Adventists as cults for their "un-Christian" unorthodox beliefs. This is a wrong path to go down because while doing so, these leaders are forgetting the fundamentalist movement of true Christianity of late 19th and early 20th centuries that were trying to apologetically and evangelistically overcome liberal progressive Christianity. That battle for the Christian faith and the Bible was lost. Now, today the word "fundamentalist" is an equivalent to the term "cult." When so-called true, genuine Christianity has had a far worse history, similarly many mistaken doctrinal positions, have done some mind control of their own, have divided into tens of thousands of denominations that all believe differently, it might not be wise to call other religious groups a cult. If you find these insights offense, it might be a little mind control at work, so ponder things objectively.

This is no easy task for most Christians. The Jehovah's Witnesses are well trained to defend their beliefs. They spend five meetings a week, much personal study and meeting preparation in taking in what they believe and learning how to defend their version of the faith. This is not said to scare anyone off from trying to approach the Witnesses, but rather to encourage you to prepare well. The irony is; we do not have to go out and find the

Witnesses, as they come to us because they go house-to-house. The objective is not to be confrontational, as Witnesses are trained to abandon such conversations.

The best thing we can do is know what we believe very well and be accomplished at defending it. It is best to know what they believe as well and what Scriptures they use to defend such views. However, it is not that simple because they will know what we believe and what verses we use, and they will be prepared to undermine those verses. As was said, it is not going to be easy. It gets worse still if the average Witness cannot deal with our preparedness, but they believe we are sincerely interested, they will bring a pioneer[9] with them the next time they visit us. These ones have far more experience and knowledge. If that fails, they will bring the most qualified congregation elder. Do not be fooled; some Witnesses study secular books; they learn Hebrew and Greek, among many other academic fields. These latter ones are few in number, but I thought I would mention it in case they happen to be in your area.

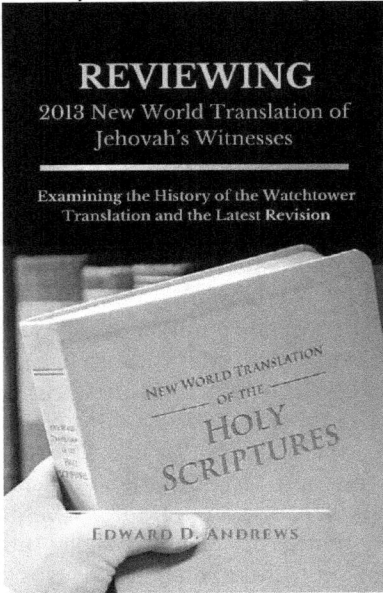

REVIEWING

2013 New World Translation of Jehovah's Witnesses

Examining the History of the Watchtower Translation and the Latest Revision

NEW WORLD TRANSLATION OF THE HOLY SCRIPTURES

EDWARD D. ANDREWS

If we want the Witnesses to visit us, all we have to do is write or call the main branch of Jehovah's Witnesses[10] and ask for one of their books, which will give us the basic beliefs they hold. They will not mail us the publication; they will have someone from the local Kingdom Hall (their church) deliver it. When they come, they will walk us through the book and look to start a study with us. If we want to win them over to our side, this is the best way, as we would have them all to ourselves in our home, going over doctrinal positions. It is best to make this stipulation, though, "I will study your book with you, but as you know, I believe differently, so

---

[9] An auxiliary pioneer is a Witness, who spends 50-hours a month out evangelizing. A regular pioneer is a Witness, who spends 70-hours a month out evangelizing. It used to be 70-hours for the auxiliary and 90 hours for the regular pioneer. They also have a special pioneer that spends 120 hours a month.

[10] Jehovah's Witnesses
25 Columbia Heights
BROOKLYN NY 11201-2483
UNITED STATES
+1 718-560-5000

along the way, I may raise objections, ask for more proof, as well as share how I see whatever we may be discussing." They will agree to this stipulation because they always believe they have the upper hand.

The best approach is to agree where there is an agreement because believe it or not; there will be more agreement than one might imagine. When we come to points of disagreement, have them make their case, letting them get through the entire presentation and then undermine it with Scripture from their New World Translation. We can be prepared because they will give us a copy of the book to prepare for the study; they will also provide us with a New World Translation if we ask for one. As we prepare for the study, be prepared to be surprised because the Witness literature is excellent at using verses based on isolated reading sound as though they do support what is being said in their publications. Thus, we need to look the verses up in three literal translations (NASB, ESV, and HCSB), we need to read the section of Scripture that the text is found in and look it up in a commentary volume. A superb, easy to read commentary volume set is Holman Old and New Testament Commentary Volumes. If there are translation issues, we need to investigate these. If there are textual issues, we need to examine these.

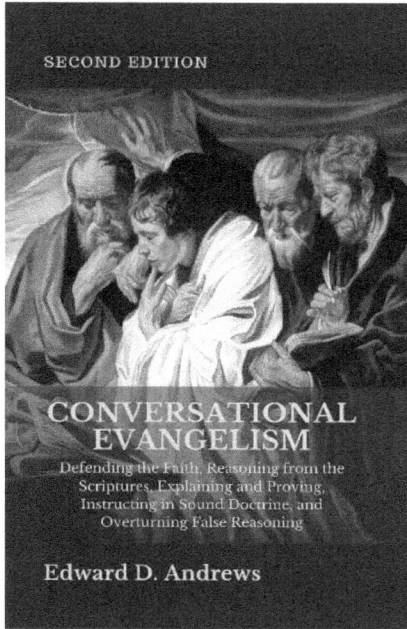

Once they arrive for the study, we should have our legal pad or our tablet right beside us with our information. Once we complete the study, let the Witness know that we take issue with some of the verses that they had used to support their position. Then, go through them one by one. It is as simple as that. If we share this information without asking them to defend against it, over the course of their study book (4-6 months), they will begin to doubt their position. One cannot sit through one correction after another over so many months and not begin to wonder about whether they are in the right religion. One thing that we do not want to do is what many of the cult books that undermine the Witnesses beliefs recommend, i.e., shock and awe. They want us to sit there, accept a Witness belief, and methodically undermine it. This will not work; the Witness will not open,

SECOND EDITION

THE EVANGELISM HANDBOOK

How All Christians Can Effectively
Share God's Word in Their
Community

Matthew 9:37-38: Then he said to his disciples, "The harvest is
plentiful, but the laborers are few. Therefore beg the Master of the
harvest to send out workers into his harvest."

Matthew 24:14; 28:18-20: Jesus said, "this gospel of the kingdom will
be proclaimed in all the inhabited earth." "... Go therefore and make
disciples of all nations ... teaching them ..."

Edward D. Andrews

look in, or be a part of such a book. Even if we do not show them the book, they will walk out if the situation looks like an assault on their faith. I apologize for this analogy, but one can cook an animal alive if they turn up the heat slowly enough. If we walk through a couple of their books over an extended period, it will be so slow of an undermining that it will not be an affront, an assault.

REASONING 4 What Will You Say to a Muslim?

Have you ever had the opportunity of sharing God's Word with a Muslim? If you have or if you have seen them on a news program being interviewed, you likely noticed that they a fervent, intense, passionate, zealous belief in God. The apostle Paul told Timothy, "This is good, and it is acceptable in the sight of God our Savior, who desires all men to be saved and to come to an accurate knowledge[11] of truth." (1 Tim. 2:3-4) The following basic information should be helpful in your pursuit to witness to all kinds of people, in this case, Muslims. However, first, we recommend a few books.

Books to Help You Explain Your Belief

- IS THE QURAN THE WORD OF GOD?: Is Islam the One True Faith?

- UNDERSTANDING ISLAM AND TERRORISM: A Biblical Point of View

- A CHRISTIAN'S GUIDE TO ISLAM: What Every Christian Needs to Know About Islam and the Rise of Radical Islam

Many have not had many opportunities to witness to a Muslim. Most of us because of radical Islam (e.g., ISIS and Al Qaeda) over the past 15-years have gotten to know that quite a number of Muslims have a radical belief in Allah, the Islamic name of God. However, most Muslims are not that familiar with what the Bible truly teaches. It is our hope that we can share our faith with Muslims when the opportunity presents itself. The following is a simple introduction to that process. For more on this subject, please see the above books

Islamic Worldview

A worldview in the simplest terms is "the sum total of a person's answers to the most important questions in life."[12] Ironically, in today's world, while everyone has a worldview, most are unaware of what it is and how it may affect their lives. For this reason, most worldviews are deficient, contradictory, and seldom are they united in thought with their many different pieces. (Nash 1999, 13)

---

[11] *Epignosis* is a strengthened or intensified form of *gnosis* (*epi*, meaning "additional"), meaning, "true," "real," "full," "complete" or "accurate," depending upon the context. Paul and Peter alone use *epignosis*.

[12] Zondervan (2010-06-19). Life's Ultimate Questions: An Introduction to Philosophy. Zondervan. Kindle Edition.

IS THE QURAN THE WORD OF GOD?

☪

Is Islam the One True Faith?

Edward D. Andrews

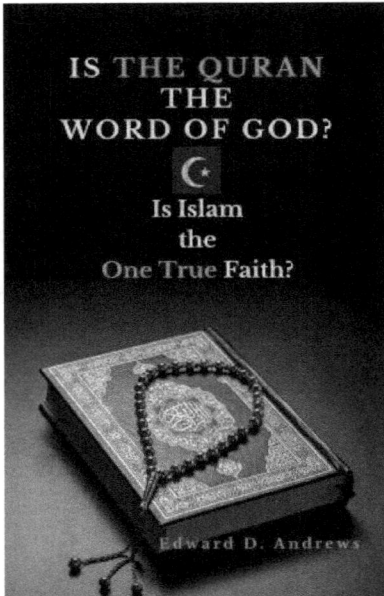

While most of the earth's seven billion residents are walking around unaware of the fact that they are carrying an insufficient worldview; it actually affects every facet of their life. Moreover, it is actually a matter of life and death that one not only become better aware of their worldview. However, it must be brought into alignment with the only worldview that matter, the thinking of the Creator of humankind himself as he has revealed to us through his loving revelation, the Bible.

What is of supreme importance then, is that the Christians continuously evaluate their own worldview, making sure that it is in harmony with God's Word. Nevertheless, it is just as important to familiarize ourselves with the worldview of others: Buddhism, Hinduism, Shintoism, and Islam, to mention a few. "Converts and immigrant [of Islamic] communities are found in almost every part of the world. With about 1.62 billion followers or 23% of the global population, Islam is the second-largest religion by a number of adherents and, according to many sources, the fastest-growing major religion in the world."[13]

Evangelism is the obligation of every Christian, to teach and preach the gospel to the ends of the earth. (Matt 24:14; 28:19-20; Ac 1:8) It is for this reason that we will look at the worldview of Islam and contrast it with the Christian belief system. Initially, we will offer a brief overview of how Islam got its start and explain some terms that should help us better understand the Islamic mindset. Next, we will look at a short overview of five facets that every worldview possesses: Islam's view of God, view reality, knowledge, moral code, and religious character. Finally, we will contrast the beliefs systems of Islam with Christianity before ending with a brief overview of what has been said herein.

Short Overview of Islam[14]

Muhammad bin [son of] Abdullah, was born about 570 C.E., in the prosperous trade city of Mecca. Young Muhammad was very much

---

[13] Islam – Wikipedia, the free encyclopedia, http://en.wikipedia.org/wiki/Islam(accessed September 14, 2015).

[14] [Ar *islām* submission (to the will of God)] 1817.—*Merriam-Webster's Collegiate Dictionary.* Eleventh ed. Springfield, Mass.: Merriam-Webster, Inc., 2003

dissatisfied with the religious system of his day, it became known as the 'time of ignorance.' His people were steeped in idolatry and the worship of hundreds of local deities. Muhammad through his interactions with local Christian and Jewish traders had become just as disappointed with their approach to God as well. As far as he was concerned, both Judaism and Christianity had abandoned Allah,[15] and for this reason, the God of the Bible was raising up one last prophet to restore the pure religion of Abraham.

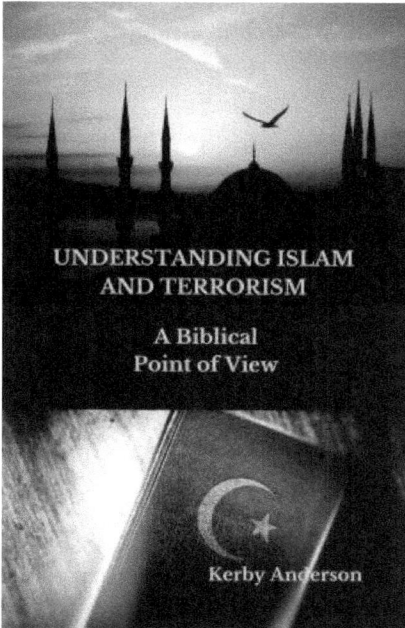

UNDERSTANDING ISLAM AND TERRORISM

A Biblical Point of View

Kerby Anderson

According to *A Christian's Pocket Guide to Islam* "the Jews, the Arabs gained a superficial knowledge of the Old Testament stories and Jewish folklore, which is seen in the pages of the Quran. The Christianity that Muhammad encountered was brought to Arabia chiefly by Christians who had fled from the Byzantine Empire, victims of the intricate Christological controversies of those days, who had been condemned as heretics. Muhammad's very imperfect understanding of Christian doctrine was probably due to the nature of these informants." (Sookhdeo 2001, 10)

Muhammad's marriage into a wealthy family afforded him the opportunity to engage in meditative thought as to his religious environment. It was on one of these occasioned trips that Allah or Gabriel began to come to him while he was in his trance. The inhabitants of Mecca were not receptive to these visions, believing Muhammad to be "demon-possessed." It is at this point, about 622 C.E.; Muhammad made his flight to Medina. This also corresponds with the start of the Muslim[16] calendar. As a result, dates are known as A.H.[17] (Sookhdeo 2001, 12, 80)

---

[15] (Arab. *Allāh*, a contraction of *al-Ilāh*, "the God")—*The Encyclopedia of Christianity*, 749

[16] [Ar *muslim*, lit., one who submits (to God)] ca.1615—*Merriam-Webster's Collegiate Dictionary.* Eleventh ed. Springfield, Mass.: Merriam-Webster, Inc., 2003

[17] Anno Hegirae, year of the flight

The Arabic word *jihad*[18] was given birth to in about 624 C.E. after the battle of Badr, in which it was decided that the Muslim had an obligation to perform a jihad whenever they perceived a threat of any sort. Further, it was here in Medina that the Quran, a sacred textbook, was further developed into the final revelation from Allah. It is here too that many of the traditions of Islam had their beginning: prayer toward Jerusalem, Friday as the day of worship, and the fast of Ramadan.[19] In Muhammad's lifetime, he managed to conquer all of Arabia, being the first to unite all Muslims as one, into the religion of Islam. Muhammad died in 632 C.E. and was succeeded by Caliph[20] Abu Bakr in 634 C.E. and Caliph Umar in 644 C.E. Throughout this initial period of unity, Syria, Iraq, Persia, and Egypt fell to the newly founded Islamic empire. (Sookhdeo 2001, 13)

There are the two major divisions of Islam, the Sunni and the Shiah. This came apart back at the time of Muhammad's successors and is based on a discrepancy of understanding as to who is his lawful religious heirs. Does the procession come after Muhammad's lineage as the Shiite Muslims assert or is it based on the elective office as the majority Sunni claim? The argument continues to this day, with no resolution in sight. The Sunni Muslims are in the majority by about ninety percent, with most of the ten percent of Shiah being found in Iran. Of course, with the Shiah being in the minority, they are under constant persecution by the Sunnis. (Sookhdeo 2001, 65)

Five Facets of the Islamic Worldview[21]

Unlike most of the religious systems that exist today, Islam has accomplished a way of life that many other institutions only dream of, a unity to the point that the Quran and the hadith[22] govern their religious

---

[18] [Ar *jihād*] 1869: a holy war waged on behalf of Islam as a religious duty *also*: a personal struggle in devotion to Islam esp. involving spiritual discipline—ibid.

[19] [Ar *Ramaḍān*] ca. 1595: the ninth month of the Islamic year observed as sacred with fasting practiced daily from dawn to sunset—ibid.

[20] [caliphe, Ar khalīfa successor] 14c: a successor of Muhammad as temporal and spiritual head of Islam —ibid.

[21] As the Sunni are in the vast majority, this worldview will largely reflect their belief system. The hadith is the narrative record of the sayings or customs of Muhammad and his companions; and the collective body of traditions relating to Muhammad and his companions.—*Merriam-Webster's Collegiate Dictionary*. Eleventh ed. Springfield, Mass.: Merriam-Webster, Inc., 2003

[22] The hadith is the narrative record of the sayings or customs of Muhammad and his companions; and the collective body of traditions relating to Muhammad and his companions.—*Merriam-Webster's Collegiate Dictionary*. Eleventh ed. Springfield, Mass.: Merriam-Webster, Inc., 2003

system, state laws, and all social settings, Shariah law.[23] It is sacrilege to violate any of the religious norms, and one Muslim will correct another, and in many cases, it can mean death in Islamic countries.

View of God

Allah is the God of Islam. The Quran states: "So believe in God and His apostles. Say not 'Trinity': desist: it will be better for you: for God is One God." (Surah 4:171, *AYA*) The Quran does not dispute the reality of God's existence, like the Bible, it simply speaks as though he is. For the Muslim, Allah is almighty, all powerful, all knowing, and has no equal. Allah is the God of judgment and is to be feared in the sense of dread, not a reverential fear. As Abraham was God's friend, the concept of a Muslim being the friend of Allah would be foreign to his mindset.

View of Reality

Islam believes Allah, "Almighty God" is the One who created the universe. They believe that the universe we are living in is not eternal as on the Day of Judgment there will be new Heaven and new earth. "On the Day when the earth will be changed to another earth and so will be the heavens, and they (all creatures) will appear before Allah, the One, the Irresistible." (Quran 14:48) Further, they believe the universe to be material, as the earth is under your feet, and is directed by God.

Knowledge

Aristotle's work greatly influenced the Arab world. Arabic scholars, such as Avicenna and Averroes, expanded on and built on Aristotelian thinking in their attempts to bring into line Greek thought with the Muslim teaching. Setting aside the philosophical aspect of epistemology and looking at the knowledge of Islam as it pertains to their religious institution, one will find that it has predominately been borrowed from late Judaism and Christianity and fused into Muhammad's understanding, as later interpreted by the Arabian scholars. For example:

- **Quran:** "Allah receiveth (men's) souls at the time of their death, and that (soul) which dieth not (yet) in its sleep. He keepeth that (soul) for which He hath ordained death."

- **Quran:** "I do call to witness the Resurrection Day . . . Does man think that We cannot assemble his bones? . . . He questions: 'When

---

[23] Shariah law is the immensely detailed body of rules and regulations, instructions for religious practice and daily life.—*A Christian's Pocket Guide to Islam.* Pewsey, Wiltshire: Isaac Publishing, 2001, p. 19.

is the Day of Resurrection?' . . . Has not He [Allāh] the power to give life to the dead?" (75:1, 3, 6, 40)

- **Quran:** "They ask: When is the Day of Judgement? (It is) the day when they will be tormented at the Fire, (and it will be said unto them): Taste your torment (which ye inflicted)." (51:12-14)

- **Quran:** "And as for those who believe and do good works, We shall make them enter Gardens underneath which rivers flow to dwell therein forever." (4:57) "On that day the dwellers of Paradise shall think of nothing but their bliss. Together with their wives, they shall recline in shady groves upon soft couches." (36:55, 56)

- **Quran:** "And if ye fear that ye will not deal fairly by the orphans, marry of the women, who seem good to you, two or three or four; and if ye fear that ye cannot do justice (to so many) then one (only) or (the captives) that your right hands possess." (Surah 4:3)

Christian Moral Code vs Islam

Each human that has descended from Adam and Eve have a moral code (conscience) that is inherent in them from birth, which corresponds to the words found in Genesis when God said, "Let us make man in our image." This moral code is an internal awareness that enables one to choose between what is right and what is wrong, "and their conflicting thoughts accuse or even excuse them." – Romans 2:15.

This inner moral code, while inherent from birth must be trained; if not, it can be deceptive. It can serve as a guide to one's life. However, it can become dangerous or even treacherous if it has not been enlightened under the correct standards, being in harmony with its maker. As this moral code develops over time it can be influenced for the good or bad by one's environment, worship, and behavior. It is the correct understanding of the Word of God, which trains the moral code.

On the surface, it may appear that the moral values of the Muslim are humane and selfless in nature. Even many similarities further the misbelief that the Christian and the Muslim are worshiping the same God, similarly, but just by different names. Islam believes that faith is dead without evidence of good works; God will punish any worship that is not directed at him, rights against crime against your fellow man, adultery and fornication are wrong, similar abhorrence to the seven deadly sins, the obeying of the law of the land, drunkenness, suicide, and homosexuality are forbidden.

This section does not contain the space to look at all facets of the Islamic moral code; therefore, we will briefly consider how the women of Islam are treated. Unlike the West, it is the woman, who brings honor to the family. Thus there are many restrictions on the women of Islam, in order to protect the family honor. There is an equation within Islam: the greater the restriction, the greater the honor. For example, without exception, a girl must retain her virginity for marriage. The woman must have someone, even a child, who accompanies and supervises her everywhere she goes. The woman's role in the house is to be the caretaker, and no Muslim husband would dare lift a hand, even if the wife has a full-time job outside the home. In the name of modesty, the woman is to be covered from the 'neck to wrist and ankle, as well as her hair.' The marriage is arranged, and while the female may refuse, the pressure is usually insurmountable. While it is permissible for a man to marry a Christian or a Jew (as they would then be Muslim), a Muslim woman can only marry a Muslim man. Divorce in the Islamic community is very similar to the Jewish religious leaders of Jesus day: the man can divorce the woman for any reason by simply saying three times, in front of witnesses: "I divorce you." The woman, on the hand, is largely unable to divorce the husband. The rape of Christian women within Islamic countries, while being a dishonor to the woman, it is a means for a Muslim man to proliferate the Muslim population because a child is Muslim if born of a Muslim man. While many today are attempting a progressive liberal approach in looking at similarities between Islam and Christianity, it has its dark side, and any syncretism attempts are severely misplaced. (Sookhdeo 2001, 59-64)

Religious Character

As opposed to delving into Islam's highly developed religious rituals and traditions; we will take a brief look at how Islam's tolerance, or lack thereof for other religious institutions. Actually, Islamic scholars who are behind the footnotes in the Quran and articles dealing with Islam's view of Christianity and Judaism have begun a campaign to conceal their hatred for these religious institutions, viewing them as infidels.[24] For example, while the word *fight* may be found in the writings, it actually means *kill*. The end game for Islam is to convert the world to Islam and to rule from Jerusalem, under Shariah law. This can be done by preaching, or by terrorism and killing the infidel. The words of the infamous Osama bin Laden bring this point home with a chilling effect: "I was ordered to fight the people until they say there is no god but Allah, and his prophet Muhammad."

---

[24] Suras 2:190-193, 2:216, 2:244, 3:56, 3:151, 4:56, 4:74, 4:76, 4:89, 4:91, 4:95, 4:104, 5:51, 5:32-38, 7:96-99, 8:12-14, 8:39, 8:60, 8:65, 9:5, 9:14, 9:23-30, 9:38-41, 9:111, 9:123, 22:18-22, 25:52, 47:4, 47:35, 48:16, 48:29, 61:4, and 66:8-10.

Islam versus Christianity

ISLAM	CHRISTIANITY
View of God: Islam considers the Trinity to blasphemous. (Q: 4:171, 5:17, 5:72-75)	**View of God:** Trinity—one God on three persons—separate in person, equal in nature and subordinate in duty. (John 1:1; Isa 44:8)
View of Man: While man may be may be weak, he is capable of righteousness before God.	**View of Man:** Man is fallen and sinful by nature, as inherited from Adam. (Rom 5:15)
View of Salvation: Islamic belief is that we can attain a righteous standing before God by works, and the denial of Christ's ransom sacrifice. (Q: 4:157)	**View of Salvation:** Man, who is fallen cannot save himself, and is in need of a savior, and salvation is by faith alone. (John 3:16; Matt 20:28)
View of Heaven: The Islamic perception of heaven is very carnal as they will drink wine and have sexual relations with dozens of virgins. (Q: 2:25, 4:57, 13:35, 36:55-57, 37:39-48, 47:15, 52:20-23, 55:46-78, 56:12-40)	**View of Heaven:** The Christian perception of heaven is that we are no longer troubled with the concern of eating and drinking, there being no one getting married, for we will be like angels and drinking and with our new bodies, pain and suffering will be no more. (Rom 14:17; Matt 22:30; Rev 21:4)
View of Predestination: Ironically, while Islam believes that man cannot be held responsible for his actions; Shariah law is very quick to exact justice for certain actions, many of which result in death. (Q: 35:8)	**View of Predestination:** This term is really dealt with under doctrines, such as foreknowledge, salvation, eternal security, the destiny of the unevangelized. Under these doctrinal positions, you have numerous views, but the majority consensus is that man is to be held responsible for his actions.
View of the Qur'an: Islam believes that the Qur'an is the	**View of the Bible:** Conservative Christianity believes

very word of God through Muhammad and inerrant, never attaining copying errors. (Q: 61:6)

the Bible to be the inspired, inerrant Word of God. (2 Tim 3:16; 2 Pet 1:21)

View of the Bible: Islam believes the Bible to have been the inspired Word of God, but has been corrupted beyond all trustworthiness.

View of the Qur'an: Early collections of Muhammad's writings came in several different variations because they were retrieved from memory. Around 650-656 there was an attempt to deal with this by creating a standard edition.

(Sookhdeo 2001, 25-48)

While it is paramount that the Christian, who attempts to engage the Muslim in his ministry, be very much aware of the belief system of Islam, it is best to accept that; it is very difficult to disprove Islam based on knowledge alone. It is God alone, who will help the message grown within the Muslim heart. (1 Cor. 3:5-9) However, this knowledge of Islam will enable the evangelizer to counter, explain, and overturn the wrong beliefs that may be raised by the Muslim. It should be understood that most Muslims are like most Christians, in that; they are not that familiar with their Quran, like the Christian with his Bible.

To the Muslim, Muhammad is the greatest prophet that has ever lived, and it will bring the conversation to a complete stop if it should be perceived that the Christian is criticizing him in any way. While the Christian cannot honor Muhammad in a conversation with such honorifics as 'the blessed Muhammad,' it is fine to say 'the prophet Muhammad.' Instead of attempting to dethrone Muhammad, it is the wisest course to educate them about Christ, which they do not view as being the Son of God, but rather a great prophet like Muhammad.

Islam has circled the earth with its presence, and it would be a mistake, to assume that every Muslim is the same. Many Muslims are only Muslim in a very basic sense: prayer, Ramadan, and occasioned visits to the mask. They may have been westernized and feel ousted by the conservative Islamic community. However, Islamic extremist is just as prevalent, and caution is the word of the day. Until one has come to realize whom they are speaking with, it is best to be very cautious about what is said, and how it is said. It must also be kept in mind that his objective is to evangelize his visitor, as much as it is the Christian's objective to evangelize him.

A white Christian attempting to evangelize a non-white Muslim is at a disadvantage from the start because they are lumped in with the immoral western world. It is best to address this immediately with, "I know that the western world is immoral in the extreme, and even within the Christian community, there are such cases, but would you agree that all major religions have those who do not represent themselves well?' (Sookhdeo 2001, 73-75)

Some final suggestions are to be friendly and tactful. (Pro. 25:15) Keep in mind that while Most Muslims do not know their Quran well, what they do know is deeply entrenched has been learned by rote. Part of the Muslim development is hearing the fundamental Muslim teachings repeatedly, which is part of their spiritual development. If we are to reach the heart of a Muslim, it will be through patience and understanding. Arguing with a Muslim will serve us no better than arguing with any other person over religious matters. Instead of using the word "Bible," refer to it as the book of God. Muslims also do not like the phrase "Son of God," but they have great regard for Jesus as a prophet or messenger, so avoid the phrase "Son of God" until you have a long record of rapport. It is best to witness to just one person and avoid talking with a group. Most importantly, women should witness to women and men to men. If a female Muslim were caught talking with a westerner for an extended time, her life could be in danger, as honor killings are becoming the norm even in the West. In addition, keep in mind modestly dressed in the West is not necessarily modestly dressed in the Muslim world. Some things to build rapport on are the greatness of God and the love of God. We could speak on the wrongness of idol worship, the wickedness found in the world today, wars, uprisings, racial hatred, as well as the hypocrisy of religion. If we sense any anger, it is best to excuse ourselves from the conversation as soon as possible.

Each of us is affected by the diversity of the world we live in, and it has come to almost every neighborhood. With this variety of beliefs, it is no longer the case of a Christian attempting to share his gospel with unbelievers. Thus, we need to educate ourselves and broaden our understanding of what other worldviews are, which may very well open up the opportunity for one receiving life. As Islam makes up 23 percent of the earth's population (1.62 billion followers), we have given more space to them, which will not be the case with other groups below.

REASONING 5 What Will You Sat to a Jewish Person

Acts 13:47 Updated American Standard Version (UASV)

⁴⁷ For so the **Lord has commanded us**, saying,

"'I have **appointed you** a light for the Gentiles,
   that you may bring salvation **to the end of the earth.**'"

Not only did the apostle Paul say the above words, but he also understood and appreciated the seriousness of it. After he became a Christian, Paul devoted his entire life to the carrying out of that commandment. (Acts 26:14-20) Kenneth O. Gangel writes, "Luke made an interesting transition and application in the use of Isaiah 49:6. Israel was to be the light for the Gentiles; but, since it never fulfilled that role, God sent Jesus to become his real servant and carry out that mission. Now Paul and Barnabas, servants of Jesus, have inherited the mantle and become the light (Luke 1:78–79; 2:29–32; 2 Cor. 4:3–6)."²⁵ All Christians are to observe this commandment.

The sons of Israel in the first-century responded positively to the preaching of Jesus and his apostles. (Acts 10:36) The same holds true for today. However, you have **Messianic Judaism**, is a movement that combines Christianity, most importantly, the Christian belief that Jesus is the Messiah, with elements of **Judaism** and **Jewish** tradition. This is not going to be acceptable, though, as Jesus told them we are not trying to put new wine in an old wineskin. First, we must deal with the fact of whether the Jews are still God's chosen people.

Are the Natural Jews Today Still God's Chosen People?

To the twelve tribes in the Dispersion: (James 1:1c)

The **twelve tribes in the dispersion** that James mentions are not actually the 12 tribes of Israel. We note in verse 2 James says, "Consider it all joy, my brothers," and the tribes of Jewish Israel were not James' brother, 'who were holding their faith in their glorious Lord Jesus Christ, as natural Israel rejected Jesus Christ vehemently. (Jam. 1:2; 2:1, 5) During the last days of Jesus' ministry, he explicitly stated what was to happen to natural Israel. Jesus said, "I tell you, the kingdom of God will be taken away

---

²⁵ Kenneth O. Gangel, *Acts*, vol. 5, Holman New Testament Commentary (Nashville, TN: Broadman & Holman Publishers, 1998), 219.

from you and given to a people producing its fruits." (Matt. 21:43) A short time later, he said,

Matthew 23:37-39 Updated American Standard Version (UASV)

Lament over Jerusalem

37 "Jerusalem, Jerusalem, who kills the prophets and stones those who are sent to her! How often I wanted to gather your children together, the way a hen gathers her chicks under her wings, and you were unwilling.

38 Behold, your house is being left to you desolate!

39 For I say to you, from now on you will not see me until you say, 'Blessed is he who comes in the name of the Lord.'"

In looking at verse 37 of Matthew 23, we see that Jesus' words are not those of a harsh judge, who is looking ready to punish the Jewish people for their 1,500 years of rebelling and sinning horrendously against the Father. Rather, he has tried to be patient with them throughout his last three and half year ministry. When Jesus began his ministry, all Jesus wanted was nothing more than what his Father wanted, i.e., repentance for centuries of willful sinning, so that they could avoid the judgment that was coming. Well, over five hundred natural Israel responded to Jesus' words, with thousands upon thousands more listening to the apostle Paul and other evangelists. They escaped the judgment that came upon Jerusalem in 70 C.E. (Lu 21:20-22) In verse 38, Jesus indicated that very soon God was not going to accept the worship of the Israelites, at the typical temple in Jerusalem. (Matt 24:1-2) In verse 39, Jesus is saying; they will never see him with eyes of faith unless they accept him and his Father.

In other words, natural Israel lost its favored position as God's chosen people, and this was to be given to another. Who? This new nation proved to be a spiritual Israel, which the apostle Paul referred to as "the Israel of God." It would be made up of Jews, who accepted Jesus Christ and non-Jews. Entry into this "Israel of God" was not dependent on the natural descent, but rather on one coming to "know you the only true God, and Jesus Christ whom you have sent." (John 17:3), In other words, it was a matter of 'trusting in Jesus Christ.' (John 3:16) Nevertheless, natural Israel was made up of 12 tribes, so James was simply drawing on the number 12, which carries the connotation of completeness. If a natural Jew or a non-Jew were to become a part of this spiritual Israel, the Israel of God, they would have to acknowledge, "Circumcision is a matter of the heart, by the Spirit, not by the letter." (Rom. 2:29) He must further understand "it depends on faith, in order that the promise may rest on grace and be guaranteed to all ..." (Rom. 4:16) There are many verses, which qualify what it means to be a part of this Israel of God. See also, Rom. 4:17; 9:6-8; Gal. 3:7, 29; 4:21-31; Phil. 3:3

These spiritual Israelites were dispersed throughout the Roman Empire. Shortly after Pentecost 33 C.E., there were arrests, threats, and beatings. (Ac 4:1-3, 21; 5:17, 18) At that time, Stephen was seized and stoned to death. " (Ac 7:52-60) The murder of Stephen was only the beginning, as Saul of Tarsus was to bring great persecution on the Christians in the Jerusalem area, which led to the dispersing of Christians throughout the then known world. (Ac 8:1-4; 9:1, 2) However, this really failed, as it was not long before Christian congregations were found everywhere, by the evangelism of none other than the very persecutor turned Christian, namely, the apostle Paul (formerly known as Saul). In fact, about 62-64 C.E., Peter writes, "To those who are elect exiles of the Dispersion in Pontus, Galatia, Cappadocia, Asia, and Bithynia." – 1 Peter 1:1

Written for Our Instruction

We can learn some object lessons from what God has disclosed to us in his Word. Paul told the Corinthians "these things happened to those people as an example but are written for our instruction." (1 Cor. 10:11) He also told the congregation in Rome, "For whatever was written beforehand was written for our instruction, in order that through patient endurance and through the encouragement of the scriptures we may have hope." (Rom. 15:4) The Israelites are a perfect example for us to learn. God personally chose Abraham, Isaac, and Jacob, because they were walking with him, while others chose to abandon him. The nation of Israel was the descendants of Jacob's 12 sons. They became God's chosen people, of whom he made a covenant, to which they agreed to follow. If they walked in the truth, they would be blessed by Jehovah's presence. If they abandoned that walk like the pagan nations, they would lose his presence, resulting in the difficulties that came with living in this fallen world. Whilst they maintained their loyalty, they never became victims to enemy nations. (Deut. 28:7) Furthermore, they could depend on crop growth that was exceptional year after year, as well as their flocks of animals. (Ex. 22:1-15) Moreover, they had no reason to build jails to house criminals, because they had the perfect social system. (Ex. 22:1-15) In addition, they did not suffer from diseases like other nations (Deut. 7:15). Jehovah promised them that they would "be blessed more than all of the peoples," and when they walked in the truth, this proved to be true.

Deuteronomy 7:14 Updated American Standard Version (UASV)

¹⁴ You shall be blessed above all peoples; there will be no male or female barren among you or among your cattle.

We all have the history before of how Israel **refused** to walk in the truth. They would walk in the truth for a number of years, and then they would abandon that truth until life was impossibly difficult, moving them to return to Jehovah. This walking in the truth, abandoning the truth, and repenting to return to the truth, went on for 1,500 years. The final difficulty in this back and forth was their rejection of the Son of God. His words to them were quite clear, and needs to be repeated again:

Matthew 21:43 Updated American Standard Version (UASV)

[43] Therefore I say to you, the kingdom of God will be taken away from you and **given to a nation,**[26] **producing the fruit** of it.

Again,

Matthew 23:37-39 Updated American Standard Version (UASV)

[37] "Jerusalem, Jerusalem, who kills the prophets and stones those who are sent to her! How often I wanted to gather your children together, the way a hen gathers her chicks under her wings, and you were unwilling.

[38] Behold, your house is being left to you desolate!

[39] For I say to you, from now on you will not see me until you say, 'Blessed is he who comes in the name of the Lord.'"

Just who are **the people** that the Kingdom was to be given to after the Israelites fell out of favor with Jehovah God? God chose for himself a new spiritual nation, which became the Christian congregation that Jesus established between 29 and 33 C.E. He no longer had the descendants of Abraham, Isaac, and Jacob as his chosen people, by which other nations would bless themselves. Keep in mind again; only Jews were brought into the Christian congregation from 29 C.E. (Jesus started ministry) up unto 36 C.E. (first Gentile Baptized, i.e., Cornelius). This is explained in greater detail below.

Acts 10:34-35 Updated American Standard Version (UASV)

[34] So Peter opened his mouth and said: "Truly I understand that God shows no partiality, [35] but in every nation anyone who fears[27] him and works righteousness[28] is acceptable to him.

Acts 13:46 Updated American Standard Version (UASV)

[46] And Paul and Barnabas spoke out boldly and said, "It was necessary that the word of God be spoken to you first; since you thrust it aside and judge yourselves unworthy of eternal life, behold, we are turning to the Gentiles.

Did this mean that no Jewish person could be a part of the Kingdom? Hardly! The first disciples of that Kingdom for seven years, 29 C.E. to 36

---

[26] Or *people*

[27] This is a reverential fear of displeasing God because of one's great love for him. It is not a dreadful fear.

[28] I.e., *does what is right*

C.E. were only Jewish people. After 36 C.E., and the baptism of the first Gentile, Cornelius, anyone, including the Jews, could be a part of this Kingdom, as long as they accepted the King, Jesus Christ. Jesus said, "I am the way, and the truth, and the life. No one comes to the Father except through me." (John 14:6) At Jesus' Baptism, there was a voice from heaven saying, "This is my beloved Son, with whom I am well pleased." (Matt.3:16-17) Jesus' teaching, miraculous signs, his ransom sacrifice, and resurrection, established him as the truth, having the authority and power of the Father.[29] The Christians in the first century were given the position of being God's chosen people. (Acts 1:8; 2:1-4, 43) It would be through Jesus to the Christian congregation that the truth would now flow. It is as Paul told the Corinthians, "For to us God has revealed them through the Spirit. For the Spirit searches all things, even the depths of God." (1 Cor. 2:10) It happened just as Jesus had said it would, "I praise you, Father, Lord of heaven and earth, because you have hidden these things from the wise and intelligent and have revealed them to young children." – Matthew 11:25

However, more truth was on the horizon with the birth of the Christian congregation. There had been 39 books written by the Jewish writers of the Hebrew Old Testament (2 Tim. 3:16-17), and now there was to be added an additional 27 books by Jewish Christians, making up the Greek New Testament (2 Peter 2:15-16). Thus, there were 66 small books, written over a 1,600-year period that would make one book, which we hold today in our modern-day translations. Yes, some 40 plus Bible writers were, as Peter put it, "men carried along by the Holy Spirit spoke from God." (2 Peter 1:21) The above view is Scriptural, but it is also the minority view. Most believe as Dr. Elmer Towns,

> Israel's hardness of heart. The Bible speaks of a partial and temporary insensibility of the nation of Israel. The Jews, who had the Scriptures and should have welcomed their Messiah, rejected him and called for his crucifixion. "He (Jesus) came unto his own (the Jews), and his own received him not" (John 1:11). Paul spoke of "blindness (hardness)" as happening to Israel (Rom. 11:25). Israel's rejection is temporary. The time is coming when many Jews will turn to Christ (Rom. 11:26; 2 Cor. 3:14, 15). God's temporarily setting aside the nation he loves so much ought to be a warning to Christians not to reject the teaching of the Scriptures.[30]

Elmer Towns says, "Israel's rejection is temporary. The time is coming when many Jews will turn to Christ." They had 1,500 years as God's chosen

---

[29] Matt. 15:30-31; 20:28; John 4:34; 5:19, 27, 30; 6:38, 40; 7:16-17; 17:1-2; Acts 2:22
[30] Towns, Elmer (2011-10-30). AMG Concise Bible Doctrines (AMG Concise Series) (Kindle Locations 960-965). AMG Publishers. Kindle Edition.

people, favored in every way, and they abandoned God at every turn, to the point of sacrificing their own children to false gods, culminating in the rejection of the Son of God, who said he had come specifically for them. Moreover, John himself says that anyone or group who rejects Jesus Christ is the antichrist (i.e., instead of or against Christ). The Messianic Jews do accept Christ, so most would think they are fine. However, that just is not the case because it is the **combining it** with elements of **Judaism** and **Jewish** tradition. What did Jesus say about Jewish tradition? He said you are "making void the word of God by your tradition that you have handed down." (Mark 13:7) Let us look at Jesus words at Luke 5:38, "But new wine must be put into fresh wineskins." What did Jesus mean?

The conclusion of the second picture is stated positively: new wine must have new skins; new ways must have new containers. Jesus' teaching will not survive by making it conform to old ways. A new form, a new spirit, and a new approach are required. Old questions are irrelevant. Such a message had relevance beyond the time of Jesus' ministry. In the early church and throughout the new age, to re-Judaize Christianity would have missed the newness of what Jesus brings. The issue raised here is one of the major concerns in the Book of Acts, as the church wrestles with the proper limits of the influence of its Jewish heritage. The focus is not on a return to something old and ancient, but on the presence of something new. This does not mean that some forms of the old worship, like fasting, cannot continue; but it does mean that they are seen differently. The remarks fit the situation in Jesus' ministry, but the significance became timeless for the church's perspective.[31] (Bock 1994, p. 521)

Will the Jews in the last days, or during the great tribulation, finally be moved to accept Jesus Christ?

Romans 11:25-26 Good News Translation (GNT)

25 There is a secret truth, my friends, which I want you to know, for it will keep you from thinking how wise you are. It is that the stubbornness of the people of Israel is not permanent, but will last only until the complete number of Gentiles comes to God. 26 And **this is how** all Israel will be saved. As the scripture says,

"The Savior will come from Zion
and remove all wickedness from the descendants of Jacob."

Notice the GNT says, "this is how (ESV, HCSB, "and in this way") Greek, *houtos*] all Israel will be saved." In addition, notice that this "all Israel will be saved" is not accomplished by the same conversion of all the Jews, but rather "the complete number of Gentiles comes to God." A

---

[31] Paul raises such issues in 1 Cor. 7:17–24; 8–11; and Rom. 14–15. While not rejecting Jewish worship forms, he did not regard them as required. His approach parallels Jesus'.

Manual Greek Lexicon of the New Testament [Edinburgh, 1937, G. Abbott-Smith, p. 329] defines *houtos* as meaning "in this way, so, thus."). In addition, *A TRANSLATOR'S HANDBOOK ON PAUL'S LETTER TO THE ROMANS* [New York, 1973, United Bible Societies, p. 227], says, "*This is how* relates back to what Paul has previously said."

If we are to understand Romans 11:25-26 correctly, it must be in the context of the book of Romans as a whole, and the rest of the New Testament. What did Paul say at Romans 2:28-28, "For no one is a Jew who is merely one outwardly, nor is circumcision outward and physical. But a Jew is one inwardly, and circumcision is a matter of the heart, by the Spirit, not by the letter. His praise is not from man but from God." At Romans 9:26 Paul says, "For not all those who are descended from Israel are truly Israel."

What about the argument that the Abrahamic covenant assures that the Jews will always be God's chosen people.

Galatians 3:27-29 Updated American Standard Version (UASV)

[27] For as many of you as were baptized into Christ have put on Christ. [28] There is neither Jew nor Greek, there is neither slave nor free man, there is neither male nor female; for you are all one in Christ Jesus. [29] And if you are of Christ, then you are of Abraham's seed,[32] heirs according to promise.

[27] For all of you who were baptized into Christ have clothed yourselves with Christ. [28] There is neither Jew nor Greek, there is neither slave nor free man, there is neither male nor female; for you are all one in Christ Jesus. [29] And *if you belong to Christ, then you are Abraham's descendants,* heirs according to promise. (Italics mine)

Here we see things from God's perspective; it is not a matter of being a natural descendant of Abraham that makes one a part of Abraham's seed. Are the things going on in Israel today and un unto Christ's return a part of Bible prophecy?

Ezekiel 37:21-22 Updated American Standard Version (UASV)

[21] then say to them, Thus says the Lord Jehovah: Behold, I will take the sons of Israel from the nations among which they have gone, and I will gather them from every side and bring them into their own land [22] and I will make them one nation in the land, on the mountains of Israel; and one king will be king for all of them; and they will no longer be two nations and no longer be divided into two kingdoms.

Israel has not been under one king of the line of David for well over 2,300 years. The state of Israel today is a republic.

---

[32] I.e., *descendants* or *offspring*

Isaiah 2:2-4 Updated American Standard Version (UASV)

² It will come to pass in the latter days
    that the mountain of the house of Jehovah
will be established on the top of the mountains,
    and will be lifted up above the hills;
and all the nations will stream to it,
³   and many peoples will come, and say:
"Come, let us go up to the mountain of Jehovah,
    to **the house of the God of Jacob,**
that he may teach us concerning his ways
    and that we may walk in his paths."
For the law[33] will go forth from Zion,
    and the word of Jehovah from Jerusalem.
⁴ He will judge between the nations,
    and will correct matters for many peoples;
and they shall beat their swords into plowshares,
    and their spears into pruning hooks;
nation shall not lift up sword against nation,
    neither shall they learn war anymore.

What do we find when we look at the city of Jerusalem today? Do we find "the house of the God of Jacob"? No, we do not; rather we find an Islamic shrine. Certainly, living within the heart of Islamic nations, they would not ever dream of "beat[ing] their swords into plowshares."

Zechariah 8:23 English Standard Version (ESV)

²³ Thus says **the Lord** of hosts: In those days ten men from the nations of every tongue shall take hold of the robe of a Jew, saying, 'Let us go with you, for we have heard that God is with you.'"

Zechariah 8:23 American Standard Version (ASV)

²³ Thus says **Jehovah** of hosts: In those days it shall come to pass, that ten men shall take hold, out of all the languages of the nations, they shall take hold of the skirt of him that is a Jew, saying, We will go with you, for we have heard that God is with you.

Zechariah 8:23 Young's Literal Translation (YLT)

²³ Thus said **Jehovah** of Hosts: In those days take hold do ten men of all languages of the nations, Yea, they have taken hold on the skirt of a man, a Jew, saying: We go with you, for we heard God [is] with you!

Within the book of Zechariah alone, the personal name of God (Jehovah JHVH, or Yahweh YHWH) appears 130 times. If you are ever around an orthodox Jew, say Jehovah or Yahweh, and he will jump back

---

[33] Or *instruction* or *teaching*

and say something like, "we do not say the blessed name." Jews, because of traditions and superstitions have not said the personal name of God for about 2,000 years. It is to the point that it has even been removed from almost all English translations, replacing it with the title "the Lord" or "LORD." These prophecies of a restored Israel, whom do they apply to, natural Israel?

Galatians 6:15-16 Updated American Standard Version (UASV)

[15] For neither circumcision counts for anything, nor uncircumcision, but a new creation. [16] And as for all who walk by this rule, peace and mercy be upon them, and upon **the Israel of God**.

This "Israel of God" is not based on the requirements that Abraham had received from God, i.e., all males having to be circumcised. Instead, as was stated in 3:26-29, "there are neither Jew nor Greek, ... for you are all one in Christ Jesus. **29** And *if you belong to Christ, then you are Abraham's descendants*, heirs according to promise."

The Average Jewish Person

It should be noted that the average Jew we might run into is generally a faithful follower of the traditions of Rabbis, and doctrinal views are likely not of interest. Somewhat like the Catholic Church viewing the word of the pope to be equal to Scripture, this would be true of the average Jew and Rabbi traditions. Therefore, while we might have thought we could have had some deep Bible discussion to build rapport, this is unlikely. In addition, the word "Bible" is generally viewed as a Christian book. It is for this reason; it is best to talk of the Hebrew Scriptures, even the "Torah." If anyone can read biblical Hebrew, which I know there are a limited number, his or her success of reading from the Hebrew Scriptures directly would be very successful with the Orthodox Jews, who will seldom give a Christian the time of day.

Well, we might be wondering just what can we talk about with the average Jewish person. They hold to the fact that there is one God, monotheism, who is interested in the welfare of his creation. However, it is best not to use the personal name of God ("Jehovah" or "Yahweh"), as one of their traditions is that the divine name should not be pronounced. They, like Christians, believe that God has involved himself in human history and continued to do so. Some Jewish people struggle with why God would allow the atrocities of six million Jews being slaughtered during the Holocaust of World War II.[34] Most are aware of the history of the Hebrew Scriptures, which makes for many talking points.

---

[34] http://www.christianpublishers.org/suffering-evil-why-god

Of course, it is best to stay away from Jesus being divine, but many Jews do see Jesus as a prophet. It might be best not to refer to him as the Messiah, even though that is the Hebrew transliteration and preferable to "Christ." The reason is the Jewish people are still awaiting the Messiah. This deep discussion would have to wait until we have talked with someone many times and have built up much rapport and trust. It would be better, to begin with, such ones as Noah, Abraham and Moses, and their role in Jewish history and how it affects us today.

When the time comes to address Jesus as the Messiah, we would want, to begin with, Deuteronomy 18:15 (UASV), which reads, "Jehovah your God will raise up for you a prophet like me from among you, from your brothers to him you shall listen." Then, ask the person, "Who was it that Moses was thinking of when he spoke of a prophet like himself?" "How should this prophecy be understood?" [Allow for an answer] Ask/state, "You would agree that Moses was speaking of a specific, special individual, right?" [Allow for an answer] I know some Jewish scholars have held that Moses was just making a general comment about God's intention to rise up many coming prophets, but the Hebrew word for prophet (navi) is in the singular is it not?" [Allow for an answer] "This coming one is being compared to Moses in what way?" [Allow for an answer] Then, have him read the closing words of Deuteronomy,

Deuteronomy 34:10-12 Updated American Standard Version (UASV)

¹⁰ Since that time no prophet has risen in Israel like Moses, whom Jehovah knew face to face, ¹¹ for all the signs and wonders which Jehovah sent him to perform in the land of Egypt against Pharaoh, all his servants, and all his land, ¹² and for the mighty hand³⁵ and for all the great wonders which Moses performed in the sight of all Israel.

Ask him if he would agree that is was like the Joshua, the son of Nun, who recorded these words about Moses. [Allow for an answer] Ask, if he feels that Joshua, who too was a great leader in Israel, viewed himself as the coming prophet like Moses. [Allow for an answer] Ask again, "what do you think Moses meant that God would raise up a prophet like Moses?" "In other words, what was it about Moses that this coming one would resemble?" [Allow for an answer]

We could then delve into how Moses was a great leader; he was a representative of God, "a prophet, a miracle worker, a teacher, and a judge."³⁶ We could ask a series of leading question. What did Jeremiah promise at 31:31-34? (Read)

---

³⁵ I.e., *mighty power*

³⁶ Crucifixion or Cruci-Fiction ? (genesis, quotes, baptize .., http://www.city-data.com/forum/religion-spirituality/507377-crucifixion-cruci-fi (accessed September 16, 2015).

Jeremiah 31:31-34 Updated American Standard Version (UASV)

³¹ "Behold, days are coming," declares Jehovah, "when I will make a new covenant with the house of Israel and with the house of Judah, ³² not like the covenant which I made with their fathers in the day I took them by the hand to bring them out of the land of Egypt, My covenant which they broke, although I was a husband to them," declares Jehovah. ³³ For this is the covenant that I will make with the house of Israel after those days, declares Jehovah: I will put my law within them, and I will write it on their hearts. And I will be their God, and they shall be my people. ³⁴ And no longer shall each one teach his neighbor and each his brother, saying, 'Know Jehovah,' for they shall all know me, from the least of them to the greatest, declares Jehovah. For I will forgive their iniquity, and I will remember their sin no more."

"What was this new covenant and what was its purpose?" [Allow for an answer] "When was the new covenant to come into effect?" [Allow for an answer] "Consequently, what would happen to the Mosaic Law?"

What is promised in Jeremiah 31:31-34? What was the new covenant's stated purpose? Consequently, what would become of the Law covenant? [Allow for an answer] How was this new covenant going to affect the nations?" (Read Gen. 22:18) [Allow for an answer] This type of building and leading will evidence your familiarity with the Hebrew Scripture and give him something to ponder.

REASONING 6 What Will You Say to a Buddhist?

Buddhism is a religion and dharma that encompasses a variety of traditions, beliefs and spiritual practices largely based on original teachings attributed to the Buddha and resulting interpreted philosophies. Buddhism originated in Ancient India sometime between the 6th and 4th centuries BCE, from where it spread through much of Asia, where after it declined in India during the Middle Ages. Two major extant branches of Buddhism are generally recognized by scholars: Theravada (Pali: "The School of the Elders") and Mahayana (Sanskrit: "The Great Vehicle"). Buddhism is the world's fourth-largest religion, with over 520 million followers or over 7% of the global population, known as Buddhists.

The Problem of Life: Endless Rebirth

The Four Truths express the basic orientation of Buddhism: we crave and cling to impermanent states and things, which is dukkha, "incapable of satisfying" and painful. This keeps us caught in samsara, the endless cycle of repeated rebirth, dukkha and dying again. But there is a way to liberation from this endless cycle to the state of nirvana, namely following the Noble Eightfold Path. The truth of dukkha is the basic insight that life in this mundane world, with its clinging and craving to impermanent states and things, is dukkha, and unsatisfactory. Dukkha can be translated as "incapable of satisfying," "the unsatisfactory nature and the general insecurity of all conditioned phenomena"; or "painful." Dukkha is most commonly translated as "suffering," which is an incorrect translation, since it refers not to literal suffering, but to the ultimately unsatisfactory nature of temporary states and things, including pleasant but temporary experiences. We expect happiness from states and things which are impermanent, and therefore cannot attain real happiness. In Buddhism, dukkha is one of the three marks of existence, along with impermanence and anattā (non-self). Buddhism, like other major Indian religions, asserts that everything is impermanent (anicca), but, unlike them, also asserts that there is no permanent self or soul in living beings (anattā). The ignorance or misperception (avijja) that anything is permanent or that there is self in any being is considered a wrong understanding, and the primary source of clinging and dukkha. Dukkha arises when we crave (Pali: tanha) and cling to these changing phenomena. The clinging and craving produces karma, which ties us to samsara, the round of death and rebirth. Craving includes kama-tanha, craving for sense-pleasures; bhava-tanha, craving to continue the cycle of life and death, including rebirth; and vibhava-tanha, craving to not experience the world and painful feelings. Dukkha ceases, or can be confined, when craving and clinging cease or are confined. This also means that no more karma is being produced, and rebirth ends. Cessation is nirvana, "blowing out," and peace of mind. By following the Buddhist path to moksha, liberation, one starts to disengage from craving and clinging to impermanent states and things. The term "path" is usually taken to mean the Noble Eightfold Path, but other versions of "the path" can also be found in the Nikayas. The Theravada tradition regards insight into the four truths as liberating in itself.

The Cycle of Rebirth

Samsara

Saṃsara means "wandering" or "world", with the connotation of cyclic, circuitous change. It refers to the theory of rebirth and "cyclicality of all life, matter, existence", a fundamental assumption of Buddhism, as with all major Indian religions. Samsara in Buddhism is considered to be dukkha, unsatisfactory and painful, perpetuated by desire and avidya (ignorance), and the resulting karma.

The theory of rebirths, and realms in which these rebirths can occur, is extensively developed in Buddhism, in particular Tibetan Buddhism with its wheel of existence (Bhavacakra) doctrine. Liberation from this cycle of existence, Nirvana, has been the foundation and the most important historical justification of Buddhism.

The later Buddhist texts assert that rebirth can occur in six realms of existence, namely three good realms (heavenly, demi-god, human) and three evil realms (animal, hungry ghosts, hellish). Samsara ends if a person attains nirvana, the "blowing out" of the desires and the gaining of true insight into impermanence and non-self-reality.

Rebirth

Rebirth refers to a process whereby beings go through a succession of lifetimes as one of many possible forms of sentient life, each running from conception to death. In Buddhist thought, this rebirth does not involve any soul, because of its doctrine of anatta (Sanskrit: anatman, no-self doctrine) which rejects the concepts of a permanent self or an unchanging, eternal soul, as it is called in Hinduism and Christianity. According to Buddhism there ultimately is no such thing as a self in any being or any essence in anything.

The Buddhist traditions have traditionally disagreed on what it is in a person that is reborn, as well as how quickly the rebirth occurs after each death. Some Buddhist traditions assert that "no self" doctrine means that there is no perduring self, but there is avacya (inexpressible) self which migrates from one life to another. The majority of Buddhist traditions, in contrast, assert that vijnana (a person's consciousness) though evolving, exists as a continuum and is the mechanistic basis of what undergoes rebirth, rebecoming and redeath. The rebirth depends on the merit or demerit gained by one's karma, as well as that accrued on one's behalf by a family member.

Each rebirth takes place within one of five realms according to Theravadins, or six according to other schools – heavenly, demi-gods, humans, animals, hungry ghosts and hellish.

In East Asian and Tibetan Buddhism, rebirth is not instantaneous, and there is an intermediate state (Tibetan "bardo") between one life and the next. The orthodox Theravada position rejects the wait and asserts that rebirth of a being is immediate. However, there are passages in the Samyutta Nikaya of the Pali Canon that seem to lend support to the idea that the Buddha taught about an intermediate stage between one life and the next.

Karma

In Buddhism, Karma (from Sanskrit: "action, work") drives saṃsara – the endless cycle of suffering and rebirth for each being. Good, skilful deeds (Pali: "kusala") and bad, unskilful deeds (Pali: "akusala") produce "seeds" in the unconscious receptacle (alaya) that mature later either in this life or in a subsequent rebirth. The existence of Karma is a core belief in Buddhism, as with all major Indian religions, it implies neither fatalism nor that everything that happens to a person is caused by Karma.

A central aspect of Buddhist theory of karma is that intent (cetana) matters and is essential to bring about a consequence or phala "fruit" or vipaka "result". However, good or bad karma accumulates even if there is no physical action, and just having ill or good thoughts create karmic seeds; thus, actions of body, speech or mind all lead to karmic seeds. In the Buddhist traditions, life aspects affected by the law of karma in past and current births of a being include the form of rebirth, realm of rebirth, social class, character and major circumstances of a lifetime. It operates like the laws of physics, without external intervention, on every being in all six realms of existence including human beings and gods.

A notable aspect of the karma theory in Buddhism is merit transfer. A person accumulates merit not only through intentions and ethical living, but also is able to gain merit from others by exchanging goods and services, such as through dāna (charity to monks or nuns). Further, a person can transfer one's own good karma to living family members and ancestors.

Liberation

The cessation of the kleshas and the attainment of Nirvana (nibbana), with which the cycle of rebirth ends, has been the primary and the soteriological goal of the Buddhist path for monastic life, since the time of the Buddha. The term "path" is usually taken to mean the Noble Eightfold Path, but other versions of "the path" can also be found in the Nikayas. In some passages in the Pali Canon, a distinction is being made between right knowledge or insight (sammā-ñāṇa), and right liberation or release (sammā-vimutti), as the means to attain cessation and liberation.

Nirvana literally means "blowing out, quenching, becoming extinguished". In early Buddhist texts, it is the state of restraint and self-control that leads to the "blowing out" and the ending of the cycles of sufferings associated with rebirths and redeaths. Many later Buddhist texts describe nirvana as identical with Anatta with complete "Emptiness, Nothingness". In some texts, the state is described with greater detail, such as passing through the gate of emptiness (sunyata) – realizing that there is no soul or self in any living being, then passing through the gate of signlessness (animitta) – realizing that nirvana cannot be perceived, and finally passing through the gate of wishlessness (apranihita) – realizing that nirvana is the state of not even wishing for nirvana.

The nirvana state has been described in Buddhist texts partly in a manner similar to other Indian religions, as the state of complete liberation, enlightenment, highest happiness, bliss, fearlessness, freedom, permanence, non-dependent origination, unfathomable, and indescribable. It has also been described in part differently, as a state of spiritual release marked by "emptiness" and realization of non-Self.

While Buddhism considers the liberation from Saṃsāra as the ultimate spiritual goal, in traditional practice, the primary focus of a vast majority of lay Buddhists has been to seek and accumulate merit through good deeds, donations to monks and various Buddhist rituals in order to gain better rebirths rather than nirvana.[37]

Acts 10:42 Updated American Standard Version (UASV)

[42] And he commanded us to **proclaim** to the people and to testify thoroughly that he is the one appointed by God to be judge of the living and the dead.

Proclaim; Preach: (Gr. *kēryssō*) Like a herald (messenger) who announced or made known important news both publicly (Mark 5:20) and loudly for a king, the Christian apologetic evangelist, having been officially assigned by Jesus Christ, announces both publicly and privately,

---

[37] https://en.wikipedia.org/wiki/Buddhism#The_problem_of_life:_endless_rebirth

proclaiming or preaching the Word of God with the goal to persuade, urge, warn to comply – Rom. 10:14; 1 Pet. 3:19; Matt. 24:14; 28:19-20; Ac 1:8.

What to Say to a Buddhist

In some lands, many that are becoming baptized Christians are from a Buddhist background. What is it that is attracting these to Christianity? How can you present the Gospel to a Buddhist?

Show Genuine Concern

For many of these Buddhists that have converted to Christianity, it was not some major case of logic and reasoning that drew them to Christ and Christianity. No, it was actually the genuine personal concern shown to them by the Christian evangelist and the Christian congregation. In some cases, it was the tremendous friendliness that impressed the Buddhists. For example, some have not been able to speak English well, but the Christian evangelists that share the Word of God with them were kind, respectful, and patient. In many cases, it ended up being that the whole family came to Christianity because the mother or father started studying the Bible with a loving, kind Christian. In a few cases of those Buddhists living in the United States, who converted to Christianity; when they returned to their homeland, they assisted many others to learn the truth of the Bible. – Titus 3:4

The Buddhist Mindset

Generally, Buddhists are open-minded of other ideas, but they do not consider it essential to adhere to specific doctrine. Therefore, their individual beliefs vary. There is a common theme that runs through one branch of Buddhist teaching, which says that life is full of suffering. However, by means of enlightenment, the Buddhist can stop the constant cycle of rebirth into unsatisfactory lives. They believe that if they are to be freed from this cycle of suffering, they must achieve Nirvana, which is a state that cannot be described because it is not a place or an event but, rather, it is a void in which there is no pain and evil. When we ponder what the Bible really teaches about what happens when we die and the cycle of rebirth in Buddhism, it is best that we not get lost in the forest of debating Buddhist philosophy. Rather, The Christian evangelist should discuss common problems that are of concern to all.

Focus on Mutual Interests

Generally, most Buddhists see life here on earth as nothing more than a place of suffering; thus, the Biblical doctrine of eternal life may not be received well at first. Nevertheless, every one of us is seeking a happy family life, looking for the day when the difficulties of this age will end, and know the real meaning of life. Therefore, highlighting such mutual desires can be beneficial.

Since Buddhists generally equate life on earth with suffering, the concept of *everlasting* life on earth may strike them as absurd. Still, all of us share the desire to enjoy happy family life, to see suffering eliminated, and to know the meaning of life. Note how such mutual needs can be highlighted.

You might begin a conversation by talking about the wicked world of today and how so many innocent people are suffering. Then, ask the Buddhist an open-ended question of what does he or she believe is needed to end this pain and suffering for everyone. Let them respond fully, as you actively listen to them. Then, you can share promise that is found at Revelation 21:4 and ask if such an ancient promise is comforting to them. Note that this promise is yet to be fulfilled and then ask if they would be interested in a future conversation about how suffering will end, by when and what is needed.

If the Buddhist is older, you can focus your concern on the way the world has lost its moral compass, which is impacting our children. We might ask if everyone wants what is best, to be happy, and to live in peace with his or her family, why does it seem like each modern generation has had an increase in immorality and violence among young people? Allow him or her to fully respond. Then, you might mention that the Bible foretold this before the founding of Islam, Hinduism, and even Christianity. Then read 2 Timothy 3:1-3. Then, point out that these difficult times were prophesied to go from bad to worse even though people were continuously growing in knowledge. Now, read verse 7 of 2 Timothy 3. Now, offer to talk again about more biblical truths that most people have never heard. In general, most Buddhist respect the Bible as a sacred book. So, you can capitalize on that when you read Hebrews 4:12. If the Western culture is something that is troubling to the Buddhist, you can mention that all the Bible writers were in existence long before the Western World came into existence and that their ancestors originated from Mesopotamia, which is a historical region in West Asia.

It is said that Buddhist missionaries came to Athens almost 400 years before Paul preached there. There is nothing in the book of Acts or Paul's letters that would suggest that Paul witnessed to anyone of Buddhist thought. However, Paul himself told us how he felt about witnessing to persons from other religions. Paul said, "I have made myself a slave to all, so that I may win more." (1 Cor. 9:19-23) We can do this, not by adopting the culture or beliefs of other religions, but rather, by showing a personal interest in people of other faiths and by finding common ground in the hope that we all share, as we witness to everyone that we meet.

REASONING 7 What Will You Say to a Hindu?

1 Corinthians 9:19-23 Updated American Standard Version (UASV)

[19] For though I am free from all men, I have made myself **a slave to all**, so that I may **gain more.** [20] And so to the Jews **I became as** a Jew, that I might gain Jews; to those under the law **I became as** under the law, though I myself am not under the law, that I might gain those under the law. [21] To those without law **I became as** without law, although I am not without law toward God but under the law toward Christ, that I might gain those without law. [22] To the weak **I became** weak, that I might gain the weak. I **have become all things to all** men, that I **might by all means save some.** [23] But I do all things for the sake of the gospel, that I may become a fellow partaker of it.

When we are sharing the Gospel (*euangelion* "the good news"),[38] what may seem like good news to some might not be seen as good news by others. Generally speaking, those who have good news to share are usually well received, as the listener then eagerly turns his or her full attention toward the bearer of good news. However, 2,000 years ago, it was prophesied that 'this good news of the kingdom would be proclaimed in all the world" and that a faithless generation of people would not see the 'good news of God's kingdom' and the message of salvation as very pleasing. – See 2 Corinthians 2:15-16.

The apostle Paul was sent out by Jesus himself personally to bear the good news of the kingdom. How did Paul feel about the Great Commission? He said, "For I am **not ashamed of the gospel**, for it is the power of God for salvation to everyone who believes, to the Jew first and also to the Greek." (Rom. 1:15-16) Think of how great the good news really is to a receptive heart and mind, to have survived nearly 2,000 years since the apostle Paul penned those words to the Christians in Rome. It is, in fact, "the eternal Gospel" (*euangelion* "the good news"). – Revelation 14:6.

What prompted the apostle Paul to say that he was "**not ashamed of the gospel**"? Why would anyone have been ashamed of it? It is because, in the Roman Empire of his day, the "good news" was a very unpopular message, for it contained a message of a convicted criminal, a man flogged and executed, as a despised criminal. This put Jesus in a very bad light that was not well received. Jesus ministry of three and a half years had him traveling back and forth through Palestine with good news that was fully

---

[38] James Swanson, *Dictionary of Biblical Languages with Semantic Domains: Greek (New Testament)* (Oak Harbor: Logos Research Systems, Inc., 1997).

opposed by the Jewish religious leaders. Almost all Jews misunderstood the message and thought that Jesus was saying that he was setting up a permanent kingdom in Jerusalem, which would then crush all kings bringing a reign of Jesus Christ over the world that would never end. Even Paul had this misunderstanding until he was miraculously visited by Jesus. Now, Paul was bearing witness to that name, the name of a scorned man that was executed as a reviled criminal. Now, Paul was facing similar hostility for daring to carry such a message to the people. – Matthew 9:35; John 11:46-48, 53; Acts 9:15, 20, 23.

The opposition and disdainful view of the Pagan and the Jew alike, the apostle Paul and the other disciples of Jesus Christ might have been viewed as having some reason for being ashamed. Remember, Paul now fought for and followed something that he had formerly mocked and persecuted and more than likely viewed the early Jewish Christians as shameful. He had personally been involved in mounding reproach upon the followers of Jesus Christ. (Acts 26:9-11) Now, he no longer followed that previous hateful course of action. Accordingly, he, along with others who became Christians, suffered violent persecution. – Acts 11:26.

If we allow ourselves to feel shame or embarrassment at being a Christian, we will have adopted a human mindset of things as opposed to having the mind of Christ. The apostle Paul had no shame whatsoever. Rather, after saying, "For I am not ashamed of the gospel," Paul went on to explain, "for it is the power of God for salvation to everyone who believes." (Rom. 1:16) The power of God is evident all around us in every aspect of creation and life and, it is no cause for shame as it is coming through true disciples of Jesus Christ for the accomplishing the will and purposes of the Father. – See 1 Corinthians 1:18; 9:22, 23.

The Good News of the Kingdom Will Be Proclaimed in All the Inhabited Earth

Like the apostle Paul, truly genuine conservative Christians today are disciples of the Son of God, Jesus Christ. To these true Christians, the Father has entrusted them with "the glorious gospel (good news)." (1 Tim. 1:11) Sadly, the vast majority of so-called Christian, liberal – moderate have not lived up to this heavy responsibility, and they are to be ashamed of themselves. Speaking to those buying out the time to learn how to share the good news effectively, we are never to let fear or timidity hold us back from sharing the gospel and identifying ourselves as conservative Christians.

The Father was not reluctant to make himself known through the Word; nor should any faithful worshiper ever be ashamed to be known as slaves of the Almighty Creator who gave them life. True Christians are happy to be known and recognized as those who give their undivided worship and obedience to the Father. If we are ashamed of the Father, he will rightly be ashamed of us as well. Any servant that God is ashamed of because of their unfaith course would not deserve eternal life.

Mark 8:38 Updated American Standard Version (UASV)

[38] For whoever is ashamed of me and of my words in this adulterous and sinful generation, of him will the Son of Man also be ashamed when he comes in the glory of his Father with the holy angels."

Brief Introduction to Hinduism

Hinduism is an Indian Dharma, or a way of life, widely practiced in South Asia. Hinduism has been called the oldest religion in the world, and some practitioners and scholars refer to it as Sanatana Dharma, "the eternal tradition," or the "eternal way," beyond human history. Scholars regard Hinduism as a fusion or synthesis of various Indian cultures and traditions, with diverse roots and no founder. This "Hindu synthesis" started to develop between 500 BCE and 300 CE, following the Vedic period (1500 BCE to 500 BCE).

Although Hinduism contains a broad range of philosophies, it is linked by shared concepts, recognizable rituals, cosmology, shared textual resources, and pilgrimage to sacred sites. Hindu texts are classified into Śruti ("heard") and Smṛti ("remembered"). These texts discuss theology, philosophy, mythology, Vedic yajna, Yoga, agamic rituals, and temple building, among other topics.[12] Major scriptures include the Vedas and Upanishads, the Bhagavad Gita, and the Agamas.[13][14] Sources of authority and eternal truths in its texts play an important role, but there is also a strong Hindu tradition of questioning authority in order to deepen the understanding of these truths and to further develop the tradition.[15]

Prominent themes in Hindu beliefs include the four Puruṣarthas, the proper goals or aims of human life, namely Dharma (ethics/duties), Artha (prosperity/work), Kama (desires/passions) and Moksha (liberation / freedom / salvation); karma (action, intent and consequences), Saṃsāra (cycle of rebirth), and the various Yogas (paths or practices to attain moksha). Hindu practices include rituals such as puja (worship) and recitations, meditation, family-oriented rites of passage, annual festivals, and occasional pilgrimages. Some Hindus leave their social world and material possessions, then engage in lifelong Sannyasa (monastic practices) to achieve Moksha. Hinduism prescribes the eternal duties, such as honesty, refraining from injuring living beings (ahimsa), patience, forbearance, self-restraint, and compassion, among others. The four largest denominations of Hinduism are the Vaishnavism, Shaivism, Shaktism and Smartism.

Hinduism is the world's third largest religion; its followers, known as Hindus, number about 1.15 billion, or 15–16% of the global population. Hindus form the majority of the population in India, Nepal and Mauritius. Significant Hindu communities are also found in the Caribbean, Africa, North America, and other countries.

The Teachings of Hinduism

Prominent themes in Hindu beliefs include (but are not restricted to) Dharma (ethics/duties), Samsāra (the continuing cycle of birth, life, death and rebirth), Karma (action, intent and consequences), Moksha (liberation from samsara or liberation in this life), and the various Yogas (paths or practices).[18]

Classical Hindu thought accepts four proper goals or aims of human life: Dharma, Artha, Kama and Moksha. These are known as the Puruṣārthas:

Dharma (righteousness, ethics)

Dharma is considered the foremost goal of a human being in Hinduism. The concept Dharma includes behaviors that are considered to be in accord with rta, the order that makes life and universe possible, and includes duties, rights, laws, conduct, virtues and "right way of living". Hindu Dharma includes the religious duties, moral rights and duties of each individual, as well as behaviors that enable social order, right conduct, and those that are virtuous. Dharma, according to Van Buitenen, is that which all existing beings must accept and respect to sustain harmony and order in the world. It is, states Van Buitenen, the pursuit and execution of one's nature and true calling, thus playing one's role in cosmic concert. The Brihadaranyaka Upanishad states it as:

> Nothing is higher than Dharma. The weak overcomes the stronger by Dharma, as over a king. Truly that Dharma is the Truth (Satya); Therefore, when a man speaks the Truth, they say, "He speaks the Dharma"; and if he speaks Dharma, they say, "He speaks the Truth!" For both are one. – Brihadaranyaka Upanishad, 1.4.xiv

In the Mahabharata, Krishna defines dharma as upholding both this-worldly and other-worldly affairs. (Mbh 12.110.11). The word Sanātana means eternal, perennial, or forever; thus, Sanātana Dharma signifies that it is the dharma that has neither beginning nor end.

Artha (livelihood, wealth)

Artha is objective and virtuous pursuit of wealth for livelihood, obligations and economic prosperity. It is inclusive of political life, diplomacy and material well-being. The Artha concept includes all "means of life," activities and resources that enables one to be in a state one wants to be in, wealth, career and financial security. The proper pursuit of artha is considered an important aim of human life in Hinduism.

Kāma (sensual pleasure)

Kāma (Sanskrit, Pali; Devanagari: काम) means desire, wish, passion, longing, pleasure of the senses, the aesthetic enjoyment of life, affection, or love, with or without sexual connotations. In Hinduism, Kama is considered an essential and healthy goal of human life when pursued without sacrificing Dharma, Artha and Moksha.

Mokṣa (Liberation, Freedom from Samsara)

Moksha (Sanskrit: मोक्ष mokṣa) or mukti (Sanskrit: मुक्ति) is the ultimate, most important goal in Hinduism. In one sense, Moksha is a concept associated with liberation from sorrow, suffering and saṃsāra (birth-rebirth cycle). A release from this eschatological cycle, in after life, particularly in theistic schools of Hinduism is called moksha. In other schools of Hinduism, such as monistic, moksha is a goal achievable in current life, as a state of bliss through self-realization, of comprehending the nature of one's soul, of freedom and of "realizing the whole universe as the Self."

Karma and Samsara

Karma translates literally as action, work, or deed, and also refers to a Vedic theory of "moral law of cause and effect". The theory is a combination of (1) causality that may be ethical or non-ethical; (2) ethicization, that is good or bad actions have consequences; and (3) rebirth. Karma theory is interpreted as explaining the present circumstances of an individual with reference to his or her actions in past. These actions may be those in a person's current life, or, in some schools of Hinduism, possibly actions in their past lives; furthermore, the consequences may result in current life, or a person's future lives. This cycle of birth, life, death and rebirth is called samsara. Liberation from samsara through moksha is believed to ensure lasting happiness and peace. Hindu scriptures teach that the future is both a function of current human effort derived from free will and past human actions that set the circumstances.

Moksha

The ultimate goal of life, referred to as moksha, nirvana or samadhi, is understood in several different ways: as the realization of one's union with God; as the realization of one's eternal relationship with God; realization of the unity of all existence; perfect unselfishness and knowledge of the Self; as the attainment of perfect mental peace; and as detachment from worldly desires. Such realization liberates one from samsara, thereby ending the cycle of rebirth, sorrow and suffering. Due to belief in the indestructibility of the soul, death is deemed insignificant with respect to the cosmic self.

The meaning of moksha differs among the various Hindu schools of thought. For example, Advaita Vedanta holds that after attaining moksha a person knows their "soul, self" and identifies it as one with Brahman and everyone in all respects. The followers of Dvaita (dualistic) schools, in moksha state, identify individual "soul, self" as distinct from Brahman but infinitesimally close, and after attaining moksha expect to spend eternity in a loka (heaven). To theistic schools of Hinduism, moksha is liberation from samsara, while for other schools such as the monistic school, moksha is possible in current life and is a psychological concept. According to Deutsche, moksha is transcendental consciousness to the latter, the perfect state of being, of self-realization, of freedom and of "realizing the whole universe as the Self". Moksha in these schools of Hinduism, suggests Klaus Klostermaier, implies a setting free of hitherto fettered faculties, a removing of obstacles to an unrestricted life, permitting a person to be more truly a person in the full sense; the concept presumes an unused human potential of creativity, compassion and understanding which had been blocked and shut out. Moksha is more than liberation from life-rebirth cycle of suffering (samsara); Vedantic school separates this into two: jivanmukti (liberation in this life) and videhamukti (liberation after death).

Concept of God

Hinduism is a diverse system of thought with beliefs spanning monotheism, polytheism, panentheism, pantheism, pandeism, monism, and atheism among others; and its concept of God is complex and depends upon each individual and the tradition and philosophy followed. It is sometimes referred to as henotheistic (i.e., involving devotion to a single god while accepting the existence of others), but any such term is an overgeneralization.

The Nasadiya Sukta (Creation Hymn) of the Rig Veda is one of the earliest texts which "demonstrates a sense of metaphysical speculation" about what created the universe, the concept of god(s) and The One, and whether even The One knows how the universe came into being. The Rig Veda praises various deities, none superior nor inferior, in a henotheistic manner. The hymns repeatedly refer to One Truth and Reality. The "One Truth" of Vedic literature, in modern era scholarship, has been interpreted as monotheism, monism, as well as a deified Hidden Principles behind the great happenings and processes of nature.

Gods and Goddesses in Hinduism

Shiva

Durga

Lakshmi

Vishnu

Hindus believe that all living creatures have a soul. This soul – the spirit or true "self" of every person, is called the ātman. The soul is believed to be eternal. According to the monistic/pantheistic (non-dualist) theologies of Hinduism (such as Advaita Vedanta school), this Atman is indistinct from Brahman, the supreme spirit. The goal of life, according to the Advaita school, is to realise that one's soul is identical to supreme soul, that the supreme soul is present in everything and everyone, all life is interconnected and there is oneness in all life. Dualistic schools (see Dvaita and Bhakti) understand Brahman as a Supreme Being separate from individual souls. They worship the Supreme Being variously as Vishnu, Brahma, Shiva, or Shakti, depending upon the sect. God is called Ishvara, Bhagavan, Parameshwara, Deva or Devi, and these terms have different meanings in different schools of Hinduism.

Hindu texts accept a polytheistic framework, but this is generally conceptualized as the divine essence or luminosity that gives vitality and animation to the inanimate natural substances. There is a divine in everything, human beings, animals, trees and rivers. It is observable in offerings to rivers, trees, tools of one's work, animals and birds, rising sun, friends and guests, teachers and parents. It is the divine in these that makes each sacred and worthy of reverence. This seeing divinity in everything, state Buttimer and Wallin, makes the Vedic foundations of Hinduism quite distinct from Animism. The animistic premise sees multiplicity, power differences and competition between man and man, man and animal, as well as man and nature. The Vedic view does not see this competition, rather sees a unifying divinity that connects everyone and everything.

The Hindu scriptures refer to celestial entities called Devas (or devī in feminine form; devatā used synonymously for Deva in Hindi), which may be translated into English as gods or heavenly beings. The devas are an integral part of Hindu culture and are depicted in art, architecture and through icons, and stories about them are related in the scriptures, particularly in Indian epic poetry and the Puranas. They are, however, often distinguished from Ishvara, a personal god, with many Hindus worshipping Ishvara in one of its particular manifestations as their iṣṭa devata or chosen ideal. The choice is a matter of individual preference, and of regional and family traditions. The multitude of Devas are considered as manifestations of Brahman.

The word avatar does not appear in the Vedic literature, but appears in verb forms in post-Vedic literature, and as a noun particularly in the Puranic literature after the 6th century CE. Theologically, the reincarnation idea is most often associated with the avatars of Hindu god Vishnu, though the idea has been applied to other deities. Varying lists of avatars of Vishnu appear in Hindu scriptures, including the ten Dashavatara of the Garuda Purana and the twenty-two avatars in the Bhagavata Purana, though the latter adds that the incarnations of Vishnu are innumerable. The avatars of Vishnu are important in Vaishnavism theology. In the goddess-based Shaktism tradition of Hinduism, avatars of the Devi are found, and all goddesses are considered to be different aspects of the same metaphysical Brahman and Shakti (energy). While avatars of other deities such as Ganesha and Shiva are also mentioned in medieval Hindu texts, this is minor and occasional.

Both theistic and atheistic ideas, for epistemological and metaphysical reasons, are profuse in different schools of Hinduism. The early Nyaya school of Hinduism, for example, was non-theist/atheist, but later Nyaya school scholars argued that God exists and offered proofs using its theory of logic. Other schools disagreed with Nyaya scholars. Samkhya, Mimamsa and Carvaka schools of Hinduism, were non-theist/atheist, arguing that "God was an unnecessary metaphysical assumption." Its Vaisheshika school started as another non-theistic tradition relying on naturalism and that all matter is eternal, but it later introduced the concept of a non-creator God. The Yoga school of Hinduism accepted the concept of a "personal god" and left it to the Hindu to define his or her god. Advaita Vedanta taught a monistic, abstract Self and Oneness in everything, with no room for gods or deity, a perspective that Mohanty calls, "spiritual, not religious." Bhakti sub-schools of Vedanta taught a creator God that is distinct from each human being.

According to Graham Schweig, Hinduism has the strongest presence of the divine feminine in world religion from ancient times to the present. The goddess is viewed as the heart of the most esoteric Saiva traditions.

Authority

Authority and eternal truths play an important role in Hinduism. Religious traditions and truths are believed to be contained in its sacred texts, which are accessed and taught by sages, gurus, saints or avatars. But there is also a strong tradition of the questioning of authority, internal debate and challenging of religious texts in Hinduism. The Hindus believe that this deepens the understanding of the eternal truths and further develops the tradition. Authority "was mediated through [...] an intellectual culture that tended to develop ideas collaboratively, and according to the shared logic of natural reason." Narratives in the Upanishads present characters questioning persons of authority. The Kena Upanishad repeatedly asks kena, 'by what' power something is the case. The Katha Upanishad and Bhagavad Gita present narratives where the student criticizes the teacher's inferior answers. In the Shiva Purana, Shiva questions Vishnu and Brahma. Doubt plays a repeated role in the Mahabharata. Jayadeva's Gita Govinda presents criticism via the character of Radha.

Hinduism's Holy Writings

The ancient scriptures of Hinduism are in Sanskrit. These texts are classified into two: Shruti and Smriti. Hindu scriptures were composed, memorized and transmitted verbally, across generations, for many centuries before they were written down. Over many centuries, sages refined the teachings and expanded the Shruti and Smriti, as well as developed Shastras with epistemological and metaphysical theories of six classical schools of Hinduism.

Shruti (lit. that which is heard) primarily refers to the Vedas, which form the earliest record of the Hindu scriptures, and are regarded as eternal truths revealed to the ancient sages (rishis). There are four Vedas – Rigveda, Samaveda, Yajurveda and Atharvaveda. Each Veda has been subclassified into four major text types – the Samhitas (mantras and benedictions), the Aranyakas (text on rituals, ceremonies, sacrifices and symbolic-sacrifices), the Brahmanas (commentaries on rituals, ceremonies and sacrifices), and the Upanishads (text discussing meditation, philosophy and spiritual knowledge). The first two parts of the Vedas were subsequently called the Karmakanda (ritualistic portion), while the last two form the Jnanakanda (knowledge portion, discussing spiritual insight and philosophical teachings).

The Upanishads are the foundation of Hindu philosophical thought and have profoundly influenced diverse traditions. Of the Shrutis (Vedic corpus), they alone are widely influential among Hindus, considered scriptures par excellence of Hinduism, and their central ideas have continued to influence its thoughts and traditions. Sarvepalli Radhakrishnan states that the Upanishads have played a dominating role ever since their appearance. There are 108 Muktika Upanishads in Hinduism, of which between 10 and 13 are variously counted by scholars as Principal Upanishads.

The most notable of the Smritis ("remembered") are the Hindu epics and the Puranas. The epics consist of the Mahabharata and the Ramayana. The Bhagavad Gita is an integral part of the Mahabharata and one of the most popular sacred texts of Hinduism. It is sometimes called Gitopanishad, then placed in the Shruti ("heard") category, being Upanishadic in content. The Puranas, which started to be composed from c. 300 CE onward, contain extensive mythologies, and are central in the distribution of common themes of Hinduism through vivid narratives. The Yoga Sutras is a classical text for the Hindu Yoga tradition, which gained a renewed popularity in the 20th century.

Since the 19th century Indian modernists have re-asserted the 'Aryan origins' of Hinduism, "purifying" Hinduism from its Tantric elements and elevating the Vedic elements. Hindu modernists like Vivekananda see the Vedas as the laws of the spiritual world, which would still exist even if they were not revealed to the sages. In Tantric tradition, the Agamas refer to authoritative scriptures or the teachings of Shiva to Shakti, while Nigamas refers to the Vedas and the teachings of Shakti to Shiva. In Agamic schools of Hinduism, the Vedic literature and the Agamas are equally authoritative.[39]

What to Say to a Hindu

You may or may not know, but there are many Hindus living in various lands, which would also include the United States. This means that Christian evangelists will eventually come across a Hindu sooner or later. When you do, what will you say?

Know that you do not need to be a scholar on Hinduism in order to be effective in your sharing the good news, the basics of their history, what they believe, and their holy writings will be enough. A simple, tactful

---

[39] https://en.wikipedia.org/wiki/Hinduism

sharing of biblical truths will often bring a positive response. If you are coming across the Hindu while going house to house as first-century Christians did, it is best to ask for the head of the house first. If you receive a favorable response from him, it will be much easier to share God's Word with the other family members. Some things to refrain from saying or even suggesting at the outset is that your message or beliefs are superior to that of Hinduism, or that the only true God is the God of the Bible, or that the Word of God is the oldest sacred writings. Many Hindus believe that the Bible is a Western book. However, you can overcome this prejudice by explaining

At the outset avoid suggesting that you are bringing a message that is superior to what the householder believes or that you want to discuss the *only* true God or the *oldest* sacred writings. Since many Hindus consider the Bible to be a Western book, you can break down prejudice by explaining that the Bible does not promote control over another country, occupying it with settlers, and exploiting it economically or the superiority of one race over another, and that it was penned thousands of years ago, long before the Western World came into existence. Find some Gospel Tracts to help you share Jesus Christ with Hindus.

Find Common Ground: It is quite easy to find common ground with Hindus. They also believe that we are living in very wicked times that is peaking and that it is God who will remove the problems through a great catastrophe (our great tribulation) to be followed by an era of truth (our thousand-year reign of Christ). Yes, these beliefs fit the Bible quite well. They, in essence, can be compared to Daniel's "end of days" and the apostle Paul's "last days," right before and into the great tribulation, which are followed by the thousand-year reign of Jesus Christ. Most Hindus are very interested in the topics of family life, crime and safety, and what happens at death because they see life as a series of difficult times that does not have any solutions. Thus, a common ground and talking point might be the Christian concern of the family life around the world. The Hindus know what their holy writings say about the family, but they have never had an opportunity to contrast this with what the Bible says. Another talking point might be the open-ended question, "What do you think God's purpose is for us?" The Bible's moral teachings appealed to the Hindus.

Ask and Listen: Never assume anything about another religion. It is best to ask open-ended questions and then listen. Ask questions about his or her beliefs concerning family, God, man, sin, evil, and salvation. He or she might use words such as "achieve," "attain," "overcome," and "strive." After you have carefully listened, you can find some Scriptures that are in reference to the beliefs under discussion.

Different Definitions: Certainly, there are terms that the Hindu will use that we might go astray if we associate it with what we believe it means. Moreover, there are Bible terms that the Hindu might misunderstand as well. For example, being "born again" might be misconstrued as reincarnation, the rebirth of a soul in a new body.

Be aware of biblical terminology or concepts Hindus might misunderstand. For example, Hindus understand being "born again" as referring to reincarnation, a bondage from which they are striving to be liberated. In Christian terminology, however, being "born again" means to be made new or to be regenerated by the transforming power of the Holy Spirit. It is something to be desired.

God's will is that "all sorts of men should be saved and come to an accurate knowledge[40] of truth." (1 Tim. 2:4) That includes men and women who profess a non-Christian religion, such as Hinduism. If there are Hindus in your community, why not initiate a conversation with them? Christians who take the Great Commission seriously cannot afford to ignore Hinduism.

---

[40] *Epignosis* is a strengthened or intensified form of *gnosis* (*epi*, meaning "additional"), meaning, "true," "real," "full," "complete" or "accurate," depending upon the context. Paul and Peter alone use *epignosis*.

REASONING 8 What Will You Say to an Atheist?

Romans 1:16 Updated American Standard Version (UASV)

[16] For I am **not ashamed of the gospel**, for it is the power of God for salvation to everyone who believes, to the Jew first and also to the Greek.

When we are sharing the Gospel (*euangelion* "the good news"),[41] what may seem like good news to some might not be seen as good news by others. Generally speaking, those who have good news to share are usually well received, as the listener then eagerly turns his or her full attention toward the bearer of good news. However, 2,000 years ago, it was prophesied that 'this good news of the kingdom would be proclaimed in all the world" and that a faithless generation of people would not see the 'good news of God's kingdom' and the message of salvation as very pleasing. – See 2 Corinthians 2:15-16.

The apostle Paul was sent out by Jesus himself personally to bear the good news of the kingdom. How did Paul feel about the Great Commission? He said, "For I am **not ashamed of the gospel**, for it is the power of God for salvation to everyone who believes, to the Jew first and also to the Greek." (Rom. 1:15-16) Think of how great the good news really is to a receptive heart and mind, to have survived nearly 2,000 years since the apostle Paul penned those words to the Christians in Rome. It is, in fact, "the eternal Gospel" (*euangelion* "the good news"). – Revelation 14:6.

What prompted the apostle Paul to say that he was "**not ashamed of the gospel**"? Why would anyone have been ashamed of it? It is because, in the Roman Empire of his day, the "good news" was a very unpopular message, for it contained a message of a convicted criminal, a man flogged and executed, as a despised criminal. This put Jesus in a very bad light that was not well received. Jesus ministry of three and a half years had him traveling back and forth through Palestine with the good news that was fully opposed by the Jewish religious leaders. Almost all Jews misunderstood the message and thought that Jesus was saying that he was setting up a permanent kingdom in Jerusalem, which would then crush all kings bringing a reign of Jesus Christ over the world that would never end. Even Paul had this misunderstanding until he was miraculously visited by Jesus. Now, Paul was bearing witness to that name, the name of a scorned man that was executed as a reviled criminal. Now, Paul was facing similar

---

[41] James Swanson, *Dictionary of Biblical Languages with Semantic Domains: Greek (New Testament)* (Oak Harbor: Logos Research Systems, Inc., 1997).

hostility for daring to carry such a message to the people. – Matthew 9:35; John 11:46-48, 53; Acts 9:15, 20, 23.

The opposition and disdainful view of the Pagan and the Jew alike, the apostle Paul and the other disciples of Jesus Christ might have been viewed as having some reason for being ashamed. Remember, Paul now fought for and followed something that he had formerly mocked and persecuted and more than likely viewed the early Jewish Christians as shameful. He had personally been involved in mounding reproach upon the followers of Jesus Christ. (Acts 26:9-11) Now, he no longer followed that previous hateful course of action. Accordingly, he, along with others who became Christians, suffered violent persecution. – Acts 11:26.

If we allow ourselves to feel shame or embarrassment at being a Christian, we will have adopted a human mindset of things as opposed to having the mind of Christ. The apostle Paul had no shame whatsoever. Rather, after saying, "For I am not ashamed of the gospel," Paul went on to explain, "for it is the power of God for salvation to everyone who believes." (Rom. 1:16) The power of God is evident all around us in every aspect of creation and life and, it is no cause for shame as it is coming through true disciples of Jesus Christ for the accomplishing the will and purposes of the Father. – See 1 Corinthians 1:18; 9:22, 23.

The person you are sharing the Gospel with says, "I am an atheist." Nevertheless, you still want to find a way to have a discussion with the person and offer them your insights and maybe recommend some books that can help them see that there is solid scientific evidence that points to the existence of a Creator. Does the evidence support the Bible's description of events, or was Darwin correct?

First, it should be recognized that today's atheist is not the same as the atheist of 30-50 years ago. The atheists of the 1950s to the 1980s simply did not believe in creation or a Creator and were not eager to share that belief with others. Today, the atheist's movement is more involved in sharing their beliefs than Christians are. Their messages are on billboards, the radio, and television, and they have actually written many apologetic books defending their faith, i.e., secularism, humanism, relativism, and nihilism. We have now entered the era of the New Atheism.

New Atheism is a social and political movement that began in the early 2000s in favor of atheism and secularism promoted by a collection of modern atheist writers who have advocated the view that "religion should not simply be tolerated but should be countered, criticized, and exposed by rational argument wherever its influence arises."[42] There is uncertainty about how

[42] Hooper, Simon. "The rise of the New Atheists". CNN. Retrieved 16 March 2010.

much influence the movement has had on religious demographics worldwide. In England and Wales, as of 2011 the increase in atheist groups, student societies, publications and public appearances coincided with the non-religious being the largest growing demographic, followed by Islam and Evangelicalism.[43] New Atheism lends itself to and often overlaps with secular humanism and antitheism, particularly in its criticism of what many New Atheists regard as the indoctrination of children and the perpetuation of ideologies.[44]

While the New Atheists authors write mainly from a scientific perspective, we should not assume that every atheist is a scientist. Many atheists have read the bestselling books by such authors as Christopher Eric Hitchens (1949–2011),[45] Richard Dawkins,[46] Sam Harris,[47] and Daniel Dennett.[48] Christopher Hitchens said that a person "could be an atheist and wish that belief in god were correct," but that "an antitheist, a term I'm trying to get into circulation, is someone who is relieved that there's no evidence for such an assertion."[49] Another thing that we should not assume about all atheists is that they are super intelligent and there is no way that we could ever compete with them in a conversation about science. Most atheists only know what they have read from the atheist books listed in the footnotes, which are not science textbooks.

Well, it should be noted that we have some Christian apologists who have done the work for us, giving us the material so that if we choose to have a better understanding and wish to at least hold our own in such a conversation, we can. The Christian apologists highlighted below are not given extra space because they are all around the best apologists. Christian

---

[43] "Census 2011: religion, race and qualifications - see how England & Wales have changed". The Guardian.

[44] New Atheism - Wikipedia, the free encyclopedia, http://en.wikipedia.org/wiki/New_atheism (accessed September 15, 2015).

[45] Christopher Hitchens was the author of *God Is Not Great* and was named among the "Top 100 Public Intellectuals" by Foreign Policy and Prospect magazine. In addition, Hitchens served on the advisory board of the Secular Coalition for America.

[46] Richard Dawkins is the author of *The God Delusion*, which was preceded by a Channel 4 television documentary titled The Root of all Evil? He is also the founder of the Richard Dawkins Foundation for Reason and Science.

[47] Harris is the author of the bestselling non-fiction books, *The End of Faith, Letter to a Christian Nation, The Moral Landscape*, and *Waking Up: A Guide to Spirituality Without Religion*, as well as two shorter works initially published as e-Books, Free Will and Lying. Harris is a co-founder of the Reason Project.

[48] Daniel Dennett, author of *Darwin's Dangerous Idea, Breaking the Spell* and many others, has also been a vocal supporter of The Clergy Project, an organization that provides support for clergy in the US who no longer believe in God, and cannot fully participate in their communities any longer.

[49] Christopher Hitchens' *Religion and Political Views* | The .., http://hollowverse.com/christopher-hitchens/ (accessed September 15, 2015).

apologist can have a vast knowledge of many subject areas but they cannot be an expert on everything. While one may be an expert on textual criticism, defending the trustworthiness of Scripture, another may be a Christian philosopher and theologian, while others may be a physicist, mathematician, or scientist, studying philosophy of science, it is the latter, who are focused on here because of the subject matter.

The leading Christian apologist is **William Lane Craig**. He is a Research Professor of Philosophy at Talbot School of Theology and Professor of Philosophy at Houston Baptist University. He is an American Christian apologist, analytic Christian philosopher, and theologian. Craig's philosophical work focuses primarily on the philosophy of religion, but also on metaphysics and philosophy of time. His theological interests are in historical Jesus studies and philosophical theology. He is known for his debates on the existence of God with public figures such as Christopher Hitchens and Lawrence Krauss. Craig established an online apologetics ministry, Reasonable Faith. His current research deals with divine aseity and the challenge posed by Platonist accounts of abstract objects. Craig is also an author of several books, including Reasonable Faith, which began as a set of lectures for his apologetics classes.[50]

John C. Lennox is an Irish mathematician, philosopher of science, Christian apologist, and Professor of Mathematics at the University of Oxford. He is a Fellow in Mathematics and Philosophy of Science at Green Templeton College, Oxford University. He is also Pastoral Advisor of Green Templeton College and Fellow of Wycliffe Hall. He is a leading voice defending the notion of the relationship between science and religion. Lennox is a leading figure in the evangelical intelligentsia movement.[51]

Christian apologist **Stephen C. Meyer** received his Ph.D. from the University of Cambridge in the philosophy of science. A former geophysicist and college professor, he now directs the Center for Science and Culture at the Discovery Institute in Seattle.[52] Christian Apologist **William A. Dembski** is a mathematician and philosopher. He is a Research Professor in

---

[50] *On Guard: Defending Your Faith with Reason and Precision* (Mar 1, 2010) by William Lane Craig and Lee Strobel; *Reasonable Faith (3rd edition): Christian Truth and Apologetics* (Jun 15, 2008) by William Lane Craig; *Contending with Christianity's Critics: Answering New Atheists and Other Objectors* (Aug 1, 2009) by William Lane Craig and Paul Copan; *Come Let Us Reason: New Essays in Christian Apologetics* (Mar 1, 2012) by William Lane Craig and Paul Copan

[51] *God's Undertaker* (Feb 18, 2011) by John Lennox; *Seven Days That Divide the World: The Beginning According to Genesis and Science* (Aug 23, 2011) by John Lennox; *God and Stephen Hawking* (Feb 18, 2011) by John Lennox; *Gunning for God* (Oct 21, 2011) by JOHN C. LENNOX

[52] Darwin's Doubt: The Explosive Origin of Animal Life and the Case for Intelligent Design (Jun 3, 2014) by Stephen C. Meyer; *Signature in the Cell* (Jun 23, 2009) by Stephen C. Meyer

Philosophy at Southwestern Seminary in Ft. Worth, where he directs its Center for Cultural Engagement. He is also a senior fellow with Discovery Institute's Center for Science and Culture in Seattle. Previously he was the Carl F. H. Henry Professor of Theology and Science at The Southern Baptist Theological Seminary in Louisville, where he founded its Center for Theology and Science. Before that, he was Associate Research Professor in the Conceptual Foundations of Science at Baylor University, where he headed the first intelligent design think-tank at a major research university: The Michael Polanyi Center.

Christian Apologist **Norman L. Geisler** (Ph.D., Loyola University) has taught theology, philosophy, and apologetics on the college or graduate-level for over 50 years. He has served as a professor at Trinity Evangelical Seminary, Dallas Theological Seminary, and Liberty University. He was the co-founder of both Southern Evangelical Seminary and Veritas Evangelical Seminary. He currently is the Chancellor of Veritas Evangelical Seminary, the Distinguished Professor of Apologetics at Veritas Evangelical Seminary, and a Visiting Professor of Apologetics at Southern Evangelical Seminary.[53]

The list of Christian apologists could go on for some time, as we have so many, to name just a few more, Ravi Zacharias (RZIM.org), Greg Koukl (STR.org), Paul Copan (PaulCopan.com), Gary Habermas (GaryHabermas.com), Richard Howe (Richardghowe.com), Hugh Ross (Reasons.org), and (Tim Keller (TimothyKeller.com). Many may be unaware that we now have some very prominent female Christian apologists, such as Judy Salisbury (logospresentations.com),[54] Dianna Newman (ses.edu),[55] Sarah Renee,[56] Nancy Pearcey,[57] Melissa Cain-Travis,[58] Holly Ordway,[59] Leslie Keeney[60] Kristen Davis,[61] Lori Peters,[62] Pamela

---

[53] I Don't Have Enough Faith to Be an Atheist (Mar 15, 2004) by Norman L. Geisler and Frank Turek; Christian Apologetics (May 15, 2013) by Norman L. Geisler; Christian Ethics: Contemporary Issues and Options (Jan 1, 2010) by Norman L. Geisler; The Big Book of Bible Difficulties: Clear and Concise Answers from Genesis to Revelation (Jun 1, 2008) by Norman L. Geisler and Thomas Howe

[54] A TIME TO SPEAK: PRACTICAL TRAINING for the CHRISTIAN PRESENTER Authored by Judy Salisbury, Foreword by Josh McDowell
http://www.christianpublishers.org/apps/webstore/products/show/5943504

[55] BIBLICAL CRITICISM: What are Some Outstanding Weaknesses of Modern Historical Criticism? by F. David Farnell and Edward D. Andrews
http://www.christianpublishers.org/apps/webstore/products/show/6102311

[56] http://thevalleygirlapologist.blogspot.com/

[57] http://www.pearceyreport.com/about.php

[58] http://sciencereasonfaith.com/

[59] http://www.hieropraxis.com/

[60] http://www.lesliekeeney.com/

[61] http://www.doubtlessfaith.com/learning-center.html

[62] http://graniteapologists.com/

Christian,[63] and Sarah Geis.[64] These women are taking the apologetic world by storm. They are setting a fine example for young girls, who can relish in the fact that they can prepare to defend the faith and the Word of God just as well as a William Lane Craig or a Norman L. Geisler. Why have I given you so many names and links? These are indispensable resources if we are going to defend the faith against the New Atheism. While many of the above Christian apologists, both male, and female, possess some of the greatest minds, which would seem to prevent the average Christian from partaking of their knowledge, it just is not so. Their books, their websites, their blogs and their videos are designed for the churchgoer, written on about a 9th-11th-grade level. Below, I will offer the reader the basics of what we can do to succeed in giving a witness to the New Atheist, but first, we must consider the various reasons as to why they may not believe in the first place.

Reasons for Disbelief

Not all atheists were born to atheist parents. Many were a part of some religion or another, believing in God, but over time abandoned their faith. Their faith was weakened by severe health problems in the family, a death of a loved one, or some great injustice befell them. With others, it was one agnostic or atheist professor after another once they reached schools of higher learning, which eroded their belief in the Bible or God.

A man was born with a debilitating illness. As an infant, he had been baptized into Catholicism; he had long felt there was no God. The end came one day when he asked the priest, "Why did God make give me this illness?" The priest replied, "Because he loves you." The answer was so insane, so he walked out, never looking back. Consider a young woman who was diagnosed as having cancer at the age of thirteen, who spent most of her youth in and out of hospitals. The mother of this child was so desperate; she brought a Pentecostal into the hospital to pray for the young girl because the word was he could heal the sick. Sadly, though, there was no cure, there was no miraculous healing. After her daughter's death, the most swore that she would never believe in some God, becoming an atheist.

- "I have seen many friends that I went to high school with just completely abandon their faith, and I was in danger of doing the same when I first went to college." – Chad, college junior

---

[63] http://pamelachristianministries.com/
[64] http://justifiedfaith.com/

- "No matter what background you come from, the transition from high school to college will try your faith." – Vanessa, college sophomore[65]

- A pastor's kid tells his father, "I'm not a Christian anymore. I don't know what happened. I just left it."[66]

Again, we turn to William Lane Craig's words, as he offers the following exhortation to parents, which would also apply to pastors and elders as well,

> I think the church is really failing these kids. Rather than provide them training in the defense of Christianity's truth, we focus on emotional worship experiences, felt needs, and entertainment. It's no wonder they become sitting ducks for that teacher or professor who rationally takes aim at their faith. In high school and college, students are intellectually assaulted with every manner of non-Christian philosophy conjoined with an overwhelming relativism and skepticism. We've got to train our kids for war. How dare we send them unarmed into an intellectual war zone? Parents must do more than take their children to church and read them Bible stories. Moms and dads need to be trained in apologetics themselves and so be able to explain to their children simply from an early age and then with increasing depth why we believe as we do. Honestly, I find it hard to understand how Christian couples in our day and age can risk bringing children into the world without being trained in apologetics as part of the art of parenting.[67]

Reaching the Heart of an Atheist

Many are like the above example or have other reasons as to why they abandoned the faith. The key ingredient is their reason, which they have dwelled on to the point they have hardened their hearts. If we repeatedly violate the Christian conscience that has been trained to distinguish between good and bad, it will become calloused, unfeeling. To violate the conscience is to ignore it when it is tugging at you to do the right thing. While this applies largely to sinning and ignoring the Christian

---

[65] Top 10 Challenges Christian Students Face in College | eNews ..., http://www.cedarville.edu/eNews/ParentPrep/2012/Challenges-Christian-Students-Fa (accessed September 15, 2015).

[66] The Leavers: Young Doubters Exit the Church | Christianity Today, http://www.christianitytoday.com/ct/2010/november/27.40.html (accessed September 15, 2015).

[67] Craig, William Lane (2010-03-01). On Guard: Defending Your Faith with Reason and Precision (Kindle Locations 267-274). David C. Cook. Kindle Edition.

conscience, it can just as easily apply to irrational thinking as well. If we have an issue with God, with his Word, with the faith, with someone in the faith, with injustices of the world and we ignore these, failing to find an answer, we will eventually fall away from the faith. Paul called this a spiritual shipwreck. Paul told young Timothy "some have rejected and suffered shipwreck in regard to their faith." (1 Tim 1:19, NASB) If we entertain our false reasons, our confidence in God and his Word of truth, the Bible, can grow weak and our faith can die. Just as we have reasons for the hope that dwells in us, we can also have reasons if they go unanswered or at least addressed, they can kill the hope that dwells in us.

Many of these ones, not all, simply need a solution to their reason for abandoning the faith. 'Why does evil exist?' 'Why does an all-powerful God of love allow evil to exist?'[68] 'Why do bad things happen to good people?' 'Why is life so unfair?'[69] 'What is the meaning of life?' 'Why is there so much religious hypocrisy?' If we lack understanding of an issue that is eating at us, we begin to drift away, become sluggish, become hardened by the not knowing, so that we shrink back to destruction. Just as we entered the path of life, we can also re-enter the path of death.

Our first goal when someone says, 'I am an atheist,' is to ask why. If he is open to talking further, we need to try to find out what led his reason and his falling away. As we listen to his story, we need to do so with empathy because this could be us, or it could be a loved one, and we would want an empathetic ear if that were the case. After we have what we need to make a spiritual diagnosis, we can look for a solution. We can start by saying, it has been our experience that there is a reasonable and logical answer to every Bible difficulty that we have encountered. We can show even more empathy if we have struggled with something that made us pause for a moment. After this rapport, ask something like, "What if I can find you a reasonable, logical answer to this issue that has plagued you for so long. Even if you still choose to remain an atheist, would it not be a relief to have that answer?" If he answers yes, we now have a serious job ahead of ourselves. Undoubtedly, there is much information on the issue. We must find it and the answer that we promised. Undeniably, not all atheists are going to accept the truth. However, there are many who are willing to find a response to the issue that tore them from their faith. Use reason, logic, persuasion and, above all, the power of God's Word, to lead them into the truth or back to the truth.[70] – Acts 28:23-24; Heb. 4:12.

---

[68] http://www.christianpublishers.org/suffering-evil-why-god

[69] http://www.christianpublishers.org/why-is-life-so-unfair

[70] This author has accomplished this several times with ones who have left the faith. They bought out the time and over an extended period, they finally saw their way out of the long years of darkness, and the light of God's Word was eventually a welcome sight.

Books to Help You Explain Your Belief

- God's Undertaker: Has Science Buried God? by John Lennox

- Signature in the Cell: DNA and the Evidence for Intelligent Design by Stephen C. Myer

- God and Stephen Hawking: Whose Design Is It Anyway? by John Lennox

- Intelligent Design Uncensored: An Easy-to-Understand Guide to the Controversy by William A. Dembski and Jonathan Witt

- Darwin's Doubt: The Explosive Origin of Animal Life and the Case for Intelligent Design by Stephen C. Myer

Some might feel that they are not smart enough to discuss the science and evolution debate. There are some points to keep in mind to alleviate this fear. What can you do to succeed in reaching the heart and mind of the atheist? First, you might consider why some are atheists. Not all atheists were raised as such. Many were formerly part of some religion, including Christianity. Many lost their faith because they saw the hypocrisy of Christianity, the horrific history of Christianity and Christians. During the Reformation the Calvinists had many arrested, tried, and executed by slow burning for daring to believe differently. Calvin justified his actions in these atrocities by saying, "When the papists are so harsh and violent in defense of their superstitions that they rage cruelly to shed innocent blood, are not Christian magistrates shamed to show themselves less ardent in defense of the sure truth?" Will Durant, THE REFORMATION: A History of European Civilization from Wyclif to Calvin, 1300-1564 (The Story of Civilization) (New York City: Simon & Schuster, 1980), 482.

Others lost their faith because of serious health or family problems or certain injustices that they had experienced. Why is Life So Unfair? For others, courses taught in high school or college have had a negative impact on their concept of God. Some have wondered why God would allow their friend or family member to be born with an incurable disease resulting in horrific suffering and death. Why has God Permitted Wickedness and Suffering? Another might have a friend or relative that has suffered from an illness and God did not miraculously cure the person. Does God Step in and Solve Our Every Problem Because We are Faithful? Another might have had to take a course on Socialist philosophy and atheism.

Many people who claim to be an atheist or Agnostic would really love to know if there is a solution to the problems that humanity faces, such as the poor, health problems, family discord, injustice, terrorism, and so forth. If there are rational, reasonable reasons for what turned them against God, they will listen to you. When someone tells you he is an atheist, you should first seek to find out the reason why they are saying that. Is it because of the history of religion, the education they had received, or the problems that they have experienced, or the world condition. You might ask, "Have you always felt this way?" or "What is the reason for your being an atheist?"

First, your Christian apologetic evangelism goal is not to win arguments. **Second,** you do not need to be a genius at science to describe why *you* find creation to be the more rational reason for the natural world. Most people that you encounter are not genius at science, so basic reasoning like explaining that the natural world evidences design, so there must be a designer will cause the listener to pause. Reason with them, "Imagine that you're walking down a long deserted beach. There is not one piece of evidence of human beings for miles. You then look down and see a watch on the sand. "What is your conclusion," you ask the person? The person will most likely say, 'Someone else has been there.' You reason with them from the Scriptures that the Bible tells us, "For every house is built by someone, but the builder of all things is God." (Hebrews 3:4) You reason, if a mere watch is evidence of a designer, of intelligent life, how much more so the universe and infinite evidence of design in it.

If the atheist states: "If creation is true, then who created the Creator?" You assume that for something to be true, everything about that truth must have all questions answered. Just because we do not know everything about the Creator and creation this does not mean that God does not exist. Think about this, do you know everything about the person that designed your smartphone? Their answer will undoubtedly be, "no." Then, you ask, "you do believe that it was designed and there was a designer, right?" Of course, they have no alternative but to admit that it was designed by someone. You then let them know that there is so much we can know about the Creator, and then ask, "why are you denying his existence on the one few things that we have yet to discover?" You can then offer, "If you are curious, I would be more than happy to help you appreciate some of the basics, or if you need to move beyond that, I can recommend that you read a few easy to understand books."

If you offer to talk to them again, you need to be ready. The apostle Peter says, "but in your hearts honor Christ the Lord as holy, **always being prepared to make a defense** (apologia, apologetics) to anyone who asks you for a reason for the hope that is in you; yet do it with gentleness and respect." (1 Pet. 3:15) In your preparation, do not fall under the emotionalism of the Charismatic faiths that believe all you have to do is tell the person how much you love God, how real God is to you, and how you became saved. For many rational, reasonable people, it might be best to use examples from nature to explain why it is rational to believe in a

Creator and creation. Notice that Peter not only said that we are to defend our beliefs but that we are to do it with "gentleness and respect." Many will give you a hearing ear if you treat them with respect about their beliefs and let them know that they have every right to come to their own conclusions.

REASONING 9 Seize Every Opportunity to Witness

When writing to the Hebrew Christians, the apostle Paul admonished: "Through him then let us continually **offer up a sacrifice of praise** to God, that is, **the fruit of lips** that confess his name." (Heb. 13:15) When writing the Christians in Rome, Paul said, "that **if** you **confess with your mouth** that Jesus is Lord and believe in your heart that God raised him from the dead, **you will be saved**." Rom. 10:9) One way that we can offer up a sacrifice of praise to God with our lips is when we seize every opportunity to carry out the two commands that we have been given by the Father and the Son.

We find that Matthew in his Gospel highlights two main objectives for us when we are carrying out our proclaiming of the Good News, i.e., making disciples. The first is that we "make disciples of all the nations." (Matt. 24:19) The other is that "this gospel of the kingdom will be proclaimed in all the inhabited earth[71] **as a testimony** to all the nations." (Matt. 24:14) There is little doubt of the importance of both objectives, but we will focus on the latter here. Why?

"As he [Jesus] was sitting on the Mount of Olives, the disciples came to him privately, saying, "Tell us, when will these things be, and what will be the sign of your coming,[72] and of the end of the age?" (Matt. 24:3) It is in response to this question that Jesus responded about proclaiming the gospel in all the inhabited earth. The question that is often overlooked is this, was Jesus speaking about making disciples at Matthew 24:14? No. Look again, "this gospel of the kingdom will be proclaimed in all the inhabited earth **as a testimony** to all the nations." The proclaiming of the good news earth wide is an important feature of the sign of Jesus second coming.

While our goal is **always** to make disciples, we must remember that most of the earth's people will have **unreceptive hearts** when it comes to our proclaiming of the good news; however, we are carrying out the second great commission that Jesus gave us, that of giving "**a testimony** to

---

[71] Or *in the whole world*

[72] **Presence; Coming:** (Gr. *parousia*) The Greek word literally means," which is derived from *para*, meaning "with," and *ousia*, meaning "being." It denotes both an "arrival" and a consequent "presence with." Depending on the context, it can mean "presence," "arrival," "appearance," or "coming." In some contexts, this word is describing the presence of Jesus Christ in the last days, i.e., from his ascension in 33 C.E. up unto his second coming, with the emphasis being on his second coming, the end of the age of Satan's reign of terror over the earth. We do not know the day nor the hours of this second coming. (Matt 24:36) It covers a marked period of time with the focus on the end of that period. – Matt. 24:3, 27, 37, 39; 1 Cor. 15:23; 16:17; 2 Cor. 7:6-7; 10:10; Php 1:26; 2:12; 1 Thess. 2:19; 3:13; 4:15; 5:2.

all the nations." Even if the people's hearts are not receptive, they will be well aware of what we are doing, which is carrying out and fulfilling Jesus' prophecy. (Isa. 52:7; Rev. 14:6-7) What a privilege our heavenly Father has given us to not only **make disciples** but to give "**a testimony** to all the nations." – 2 Corinthians 2:15-17.

As we go about our business every day, most of us come into contact with many other people. If we stay alert so as to recognize opportunities that we come across; then, we can make an effort to share God's Word, we should be able to sow many seeds of biblical truths through informal witnessing, which is unplanned witnessing that you are prepared for because you have a history of consistent, regular personal Bible study and preparing for Christian meetings. This brief opportunity that happens to you on any given day need not require some extensive conversation but rather may only need to be a brief comment or a question of interest that requires one to ponder. This alone could ignite into a conversation that will give you an opportunity to share a few Bible verses and a good message about the Scriptures. Depending on the and the reaction of the person, you may even be able to get contact information for another conversation.

Preparing for the Unplanned

If we are going to be successful in our informal witnessing, we must be prepared for the unplanned. This means some effort on your part. First, a Christian life of regular personal Bible study is of great necessity because it means that we will (1) be familiar with the Bible as a whole, (2) be about to reason from the Scriptures and defend the Word of God, (3) be able to explain biblical beliefs, and (4) persuade or convince or cause others to adopt a certain position, view, belief, or course of action. You convince or persuade another, by bringing about a change of mind by means of sound, logical reasoning. You convince or persuade another to adopt a new belief and to act on that belief.

We know what we are doing each day, so in some ways, we can analyze what type of people we might be coming into contact with that day, which will allow us to consider what we might say to such ones to initiate a conversation. We need to be mentally prepared, which will calm us and make it much easier to talk with others informally about God's Word. We now have software apps on the smartphones that allow us to bring up a Bible verse within seconds in many different translations and even Bible software that may highlight original language words that give even deeper insight into the verse we are sharing. Of course, informal witnesses are generally very brief and only goes longer if the person is the one with serious interest. Unless the unbeliever is showing much interest,

90

we keep it brief, simply wetting their appetite, so as to not weigh them down with more than they can process.

We should stay up to date on local, current affairs as well as worldwide events that can give us talking points. Many unbelievers are truly interested in how the Bible, a book penned 2,000 (NT) to 3,500 (OT) years ago, relates to current events and can be applied in our lives today. The more aware we are of the troubles our world is facing, we can be confident in introducing a subject that will have broad appeal.

Take the Initiative

If you think about it, you can turn any moment of contact with another into a Bible discussion: doctor's waiting room, store checkout line, public transportation, bus stop, when a repairman visits your house, work, school, events, and so on. In your own home when salesmen, deliverymen, neighbors, relatives, and others visit them.

Heartfelt appreciation for the truths of God's Word and an appreciation of the importance of our times in these last days should move you to embrace every opportunity to share with others the incredible message of hope that you have. (1 Pet. 3:15) May you continue to take advantage of every occasion to sow seeds of biblical truth through informal witnessing. — Matt. 24:14.

REASONING 10 Effectively Communicating with Others

Whether you are gathering to go out into your community, to share the good news with the locals, or you are just staying at the church to make calls, your frame of mind is important. If you have a negative attitude that day, you must get it right. You need to go to God in prayer before ever leaving the house, asking him for the strength to set aside any mental disposition that may hamper your communication, as well as help you to endure and overturn any potential negativity from others.

Negative Attitudes

The way you approach others while communicating biblical truths to them will determine if they will be receptive or unreceptive to your message. People love to share their perspective on everything, and so you are bound to hear some whom you will be witnessing to, who will offer incorrect information, irrational thoughts, misconceptions about the Bible, even criticism of the Bible and Christianity as a whole, among other things. We are the ones that must maintain our composure, because "A soft answer turns away wrath, but a harsh word stirs up anger." (Proverbs 15:1)

Finding Fault

First, you do not want to **find fault** with every incorrect statement that they may make. If you are correct everything they say, you will come across as negative. It is best to choose your battles so to speak. Then, if you **word things thoughtfully,** it will fall on receptive ears. The one you are talking with says, "I have read a few books that claim the Bible has thousands of errors and contradictions, it then listed dozens throughout." First, they are the victim of the Bible critic, so you will need to choose your words carefully.

'Yes, this is a common comment that I hear, and I would add that they are more along the lines of what we call Bible difficulties, not contradictions and errors. A Bible difficulty is something in the Bible that is difficult to understand, because we are thousands of years removed from their culture, because it was written in ancient languages, because the reader has not noticed that two writers are looking at things from two different points of view, among many other things." Then you offer to give an example. "May I give you an example?" He responds with a yes, and you offer an example.

You tell him, "If you were to speak to officers that take accident reports for their police department, you would find that there is cohesion in the accounts, but each person has merely witnessed aspects that have stood out to them. We will see that this is the case as we look at the same account by two different Bible writers." You open your Bible and have him read,

Matthew 8:5: When he entered Capernaum, *a centurion* came forward to him, appealing to him.

Then have him read,

Luke 7:3: When *the centurion* heard about Jesus, he sent to him *elders of the Jews*, asking him to come and heal his servant.

You then say, "Immediately you likely noticed the problem of whether **the centurion** or the **elders of the Jews** spoke with Jesus." He nods his head in agreement. You then say, "The solution is not really hidden from us." You then ask, "Which of the two accounts is the more detailed account?" He responds with, "Luke." "Correct," you respond. Then you explain to him, "The centurion sent the elders of the Jews to represent him to Jesus, so that whatever response Jesus might give, it would be as though he were addressing the centurion; therefore, Matthew gave his readers the basic thought, not seeing the need of mentioning the elders of the Jews aspect. This is how a representative was viewed in the first century, just as some countries see ambassadors today as being the person they represent. Therefore, both Matthew and Luke are correct."

Respecting the Person

People will have their own view, but you must come across **respectfully**. You respect the person, not necessarily their view. The person you are talking with may ask, "Why do Christians hate homosexuals?" You would respond with something like, "Christians should not have an irrational hatred for those that struggle with same-sex attraction. We are to respect all people. Anyone spewing hatred, he is not truly acting like Jesus. (Matt. 7:12) We are to reject same-sex relationships, the conduct, not the person. For those that are advocates for gay rights, this is their viewpoint, and we **respectfully** disagree, and **respectfully** articulate as to why."

She responds with another question: "Did Jesus not visit sinners and was he not tolerant of others?" You then reply with something like, "Yes, this is partially true, but the inference is mistaken. Jesus spent time with sinners, but he did not ever condone their sin."

"You are right,[73] the Bible does not condone hating those who struggle with same-sex attraction, but we are to hate the sin, not the one who may be practicing the sin. However, we are to make a stand against sin that is against the moral code of our Creator, and we are not to cave to public opinion. Our Christian lifestyle is reflective of the moral code of Scripture, and we have a right to our position, by the Creator himself. There is no reason that we should be ashamed of our viewpoint."

Good Communication

Your objective is to share the truth, without giving in to popular opinion. However, the truth you want to share will be better received when you afford them the opportunity to share their thoughts and ideas. Then, you express your respectful

---

[73] You want to say that they are right at every opportunity where that is the case, which helps them to see that you do not just disagree blindly, because not everything is always bland and white.

appreciation for sharing their time with you. You engender trust when they feel that you are listening and that they are involved in a two-way conversation, as opposed to being on the receiving end of a lecture.

Take Notice of Your Surroundings

If you are going to be effective in sharing your Bible beliefs, you will have to be observant of your surroundings. By taking note of what you hear and see, it will help you have far more success. You may be witnessing from house to house, and so you should take note when the person answers the door or comes from the backyard to greet you. Are there toys, meaning they have children? Is the house immaculately clean? Are there trophies on mantles? Does the house look like it is going through some restoration? Is the newspaper or a magazine laying there with a current affair on the cover? These types of things can be used to generate conversations. However, at the same time, do not come across as being too curious. You should make eye contact, letting them know that you are listening, but not to the point of making them uncomfortable. You may also note body language, as well as the pitch and tone of their words, helping you to know their interest level.

How You Can Be Clear

Do not rush your words, and express them so that the other person can easily understand you. This means that you should be aware of the pace of your speech, and you may want to slow down and pronounce your words more distinctly in private reading. You can practice this in your private Bible reading, where you can read aloud, speaking clearly. However, do not let this become a habit.

In being clear with what you mean to convey, this can be accomplished by not being bogged down in many unnecessary words but rather being more concise. In other words, if you need to make a point that has multiple parts, it is best that the initial basis of your argument is short and clearly written or stated. Thereafter, you follow it with rational arguments that are mentally clear in their meaning or intention, which your reader or listener is able to understand easily. Jesus was the greatest teacher who ever lived. He on many occasions took the incredibly complex Mosaic Law and made it easier to understand for his audience.

In order for you to effectively to teach someone, you must have a solid understanding of the subject yourself, to then help others understand the material. You are ready to teach a subject when you are, in your own words, able to offer reasons as to why it is or is not so. Jesus was able to get his points across by keeping things simple, using indisputable reasoning, stimulating questions, remarkable figures of speech, as well as discernible illustrations that were taken from his listener's everyday life. (Matt. 6:25-30; 7:3-5, 24-27) Jesus was also known for his taking an incident occurring around him and his disciples, which he would then use as an opportunity for teaching a lesson. (John 13:2-16)

Sadly, some Bible scholars have placed their books out of the hands of the common person, as they use language that requires the reader to hold their book in one hand and a Webster's Dictionary in the other. By their nature, these individuals are a polysyllabricator who uses sesquipedalian words. In other words, they use long words with many syllables. Sadly, these individuals spend hundreds, if not thousands of hours researching and writing a book that five people are going to read. In the Sermon on the Mount, Matthew 5:3–7:27, Jesus spoke for a mere half hour, covering such issues as anger toward others, lust, divorce, retaliation, helping the needy, prayer, fasting, anxiety, judging others, materialism. He did not use long words with many syllables here and could be understood by children, farmers, fishermen, and shepherds. (Matt. 7:28)

Jesus expressed word pictures that conveyed the riches of meaning, even today. For example, "No one can serve two masters ... You cannot serve God and money." (Matt. 6:24) "You will recognize them by their fruits." (Matt. 7:20) "Judge not, that you be not judged." (Matt. 7:21) But when he heard it, he said, "Those who are well have no need of a physician, but those who are sick." (Matt. 9:12) Then Jesus said to him, "Put your sword back into its place. For all who take the sword will perish by the sword. (Matt. 26:52) Jesus said to them, "Render to Caesar the things that are Caesar's, and to God the things that are God's." (Mark 12:17)

Effective Use of Questions

On many occasions, Jesus could have simply told his listeners the point that he wanted to get across, but instead, he chose to ask them questions. For those that were looking to make him look the fool, Jesus asked questions to expose these people. (Matt. 12:24-30; 21:23-27; 22:41-46) However, far more often, he used his questions to convey the point he wanted to make, and he wanted them to remember.

Matthew 17:24-27 Updated American Standard Version (UASV)

[24] When they arrived in Capernaum, the ones who collected the double drachma tax[74] came up to Peter and said, "Does your teacher not pay the double drachma tax?"[75] [25] He said, "Yes." And when he came into the house, Jesus spoke to him first, saying, "What do you think, Simon? From whom do kings of the earth collect tolls or tax? From their sons or from strangers?" [26] And when he said, "From strangers," Jesus said to him, "Then the sons are free. [27] However, so that we do not cause them to stumble, go to the sea and throw in a hook, and take the first fish that comes up; and when you open its mouth, you will find a shekel.[76] Take that and give it to them for you and me."

Effective Use of Hyperbole

Again, Jesus is by far the most effective teacher of all time, and hyperbole is one method that he used quite often. Hyperbole is a deliberate and obvious exaggeration used for effect, e.g., "I could eat a million of these." The objective is

---

[74] This was two drachmas paid by each male Jew as a yearly temple tax.

[75] This was two drachmas paid by each male Jew as a yearly temple tax.

[76] A stater coin, a silver coin worth two didrachma or approximately one shekel.

to add emphasis and importance to what is being said. Moreover, like other special literary forms, hyperbole imprints a mental picture in your mind, one that is hard to forget.

There are actually two different types of exaggerations: **(1)** the first being an overstatement, but possible and **(2)** hyperbole, which is a statement that is impossible. Our concern that we might have the ability to recognize either of these when we see them. Let us look at a few examples.

Matthew 7:1-3 Updated American Standard Version (UASV)

7 "Do not judge so that you will not be judged. ² For with the judgment you are judging you will be judged, and by what measure you are measuring, it will be measured to you. ³ Why do you look <u>at the speck that is in your brother's eye, but do not notice the **log** that is in your own eye</u>?

Try to picture what is being emphasized. You have a person who is continuously, and aggressively judging others, who goes up to a brother that is seldom critical, to offer advice on not being critical. A brother that has a log's worth of being judgmental to him is advising the brother that has a mere straw of judgmentalism to him. Is this not a beautiful way to illustrate how a brother, who has immense problems in a particular area, should be slow to offer advice to another brother, who seldom offends in this area? Below Jesus is rebuking some Pharisees, Jewish religious leaders.

Matthew 23:24 Updated American Standard Version (UASV)

²⁴ Blind guides, who strain out a gnat and swallow a camel!

This was a foremost way to use hyperbole. Take note of the fact that he is contrasting a small gnat with a huge camel, which represents the largest animal known to his audience. One religious magazine stated, "It is estimated that it would take up to 70 million gnats to equal the weight of an average camel!" Jesus was also very much aware that the Pharisees strained their wine through a cloth sieve to avoid ceremonial uncleanness by accidently drinking a gnat. However, they were quite eager to gulp down the figurative camel, it also being unclean. (Lev. 11:4, 21-24) How? The Pharisees were very quick to follow the minor points of the Mosaic Law, but set aside the weightier laws, like "justice and mercy and faithfulness." (Matt. 23:23) This one point makes using hyperbole all too clear, and exposed them for the hypocrites they were.

Matthew 17:20 Updated American Standard Version (UASV)

²⁰ And he said to them, "Because of your little faith. For truly I say to you, if you have faith like a mustard seed, you will say to this mountain, 'Move from here to there,' and it will move, and nothing will be impossible for you."

Jesus could have simply said that they need more faith, but that would have not made the impact this figurative comment did. He only stressed the need for a little faith in an effective manner, making the point that a small amount of faith can move mountain-like objects.

Matthew 19:24 Updated American Standard Version (UASV)

²⁴ Again I say to you, it is easier for a camel to go through the eye of a needle than for a rich man to enter the Kingdom of God."

Try if you will to picture a camel fitting through the eye of a sewing needle. It is impossible, not difficult! Of course, this does not mean that rich people are excluded from the kingdom of God. The context is about people, who have a greater love for money than their love of the kingdom. It is their love of money, which makes them ineligible. Jesus' colorful, vivid idioms have an effect so powerful that literally hundreds of millions of people have used them over the last 2,000 years.

Throughout his three and a half years of ministry, Jesus masterfully used hyperbole. Are you not in awe of Jesus' exciting figures of speech and his skill of accomplishing a supreme effect without long words with many syllables?

Overcoming Dismissive Comments

Many today are just not interested in your desire to share the Good News with them. They will attempt to shut you down with one good dismissive comment in the beginning. Your objective is to become effective in your ability to overcome or get around these walls of disinterest. They may hold up their hand, which is a dismissive gesture, and say in a dismissive tone,

- "I am not interested."
- "I am not interested in religion."
- "I am busy."
- "Why do Christians feel the need to share?"
- "I am a Buddhist, a Hindu, a Muslim, or a Jew."
- "I don't believe the Bible."
- "Everyone interprets the Bible differently."
- "The Bible is not practical in today's scientific world."
- "The Bible contradicts itself."
- The Bible is a good book by man, but there is no such thing as absolute truth."

These quick comments are meant to stop us in our tracks. These dismissive comments can be general, "I am not interested," or they could be based on the subject you start the conversation with. People have many reasons as to why they do not want to talk. Most are misconceptions.

- They had a bad experience in a congregation they attended before.
- They have taken many liberal classes throughout their high school and college years.
- They are aware of Christian history, like crusades, inquisitions, or immoral Popes in church history.
- They are aware of major church scandals.
- They have read popular books that tear down the Bible as being full of historical, geographical and scientific errors and contradictions. To them, the book is by imperfect men, not inspired of God.
- Maybe their life has been filled with one tragedy after another, and they cannot grasp how a loving God would allow such suffering.

These are some of the reasons, why they use dismissive comments. They have issues that are not well founded and need to be reasoned on further. That is why, many times, if you can get beyond the comment, you can get at what really troubles them, and help them reason through it. Below is an example of one trying to be dismissive, using the Bible as a means of shutting down the conversation.

'The Bible contains contradictions, mistakes, and errors'

Whoever makes a claim carries the responsibility, so tactfully inquire, "Yes, this is a common claim, could you take my Bible, and point to an example?" Most will not take the Bible because they are just repeating a common complaint about the Bible. However, for the sake of those few, who will, he takes your Bible, and turns to Matthew 27:5 and says, "It states that Judas hanged himself," whereas Acts 1:18 says that "falling headlong he burst open in the middle and all his bowels gushed out."

Matthew 27:5 Updated American Standard Version (UASV)

5 And he threw the pieces of silver into the temple and departed; and he went away and **hanged himself.**

Acts 1:18 Updated American Standard Version (UASV)

18 (Now this man acquired a field with the price of his wickedness, and **falling headlong,** he burst open in the middle and all his intestines gushed out.

You Respond: "Neither Matthew nor Luke made a mistake. What you have is Matthew giving the reader the manner in which Judas committed suicide. On the other hand, Luke is giving the reader of Acts, the result of that suicide. Therefore, instead of a mistake, we have two texts that complement each other, really giving the reader the full picture. Judas came to a tree alongside a cliff that had rocks below. He tied the rope to a branch and the other end around his neck and jumped over the edge of the cliff in an attempt at hanging himself. One of two things could have happened: (1) the limb broke plunging him to the rocks below, or (2) the rope broke with the same result, and he burst open onto the rocks below."

Then you could add, "Generally, what it comes down to is that many books that criticize the Bible, pointing to Scriptures, showing what they call errors, contradictions, and mistakes. However, what they do not show the reader is that there are reasonable answers for ninety-nine percent of these complaints.'

A longer response might be, "Considering that there are 31,000 plus verses in the Bible, encompassing 66 books written by about 40 writers, ranging from shepherds to kings, an army general, fishermen, tax collector, a physician and on and on, and being penned over a 1,600 year period, one does find a few hundred *Bible difficulties* (about one percent). However, 99 percent of those are explainable. Yet no one wants to be so arrogant to say that he can explain them all. It has nothing to do with the inadequacy of God's Word but is based on human understanding. In many cases, science or archaeology and the field of custom and culture of ancient peoples has helped explain difficulties in hundreds of passages. Therefore, there may be less than one percent left to be answered, yet our knowledge of God's Word continues to grow. R. A. Torrey said about 100 years ago, "Some people are surprised and staggered because there are difficulties in the Bible. For my part, I would be more surprised and staggered if there were not."

You explain that these are not contradictions, errors, or mistakes, but are Bible difficulties, which are difficult because the Bible was written in dozens of different cultures and times that range from 2,000 to 3,500 years ago. In addition, the Bible was written in three different ancient languages. Moreover, the Bible was written with the intention of human author back then, and we should not impose our modern world on that author. Today, we say in our news reports that the sun rises and sets at certain times, even though we know this is scientifically inaccurate. However, it is human observation. Today, we round numbers because it is a way of simplifying things if we are trying to make a point, like how many people living in America. We would just say 316 million, not, 315,940,341 unless we were doing a census. Jesus spoke of mustard seeds as the smallest of all seeds. This is not accurate. However, was Jesus giving a lesson on botany? No, he was making a point to people, who knew this seed as being the smallest. Therefore, considering Jesus' audience, the point that he was making, and how the mustard seed was commonly used as a figure of speech, this was the tiniest seed in that setting and circumstance.

Either this person raising issues about the Bible is going to be more receptive to the conversation, or he will ignore your insight as though you never made it, moving on to the next criticism that he has memorized. His response is a way for you to read his heart-attitude. You will not want to throw your pearls before the swine of Bible criticism, so move on, if it is evident that no answer will satisfy this one. However, far more right-hearted ones are going to be receptive to your insightful words. This brings us to our next point, how they listen to you.

How the Unbeliever Listens to Us

Getting a sense of how one is listening to us, will enable us to determine if more time should be given to this one. The person we are talking with may very well be what is known as a **judgmental listener**. They are listening to us to ascertain whether we are right or wrong and are labeling us in their mind ('that was foolish'), as opposed to hearing what we are saying. Then, there is what is known as the **distorted listener**. In other words, this one does not hear us clearly, because he is viewing us in a biased and prejudiced way ('Christians are such fools!'). There is the **stereotype listener**, who also fails to hear our real message because they are labeling us in their mind, as "just a woman," "Bible thumper," "so naïve," and so on.

Then, there is the **resistive listener**, who will not be receptive to anything that is not a part of his worldview. Moreover, anyone in opposition to their worldview is viewed as the enemy, and they will resist anything they say, no matter how reasonable it may be. They think things like, 'Why do these people not see that science has displaced the Bible as a book by man." We also have the **interpretive listener**. These view everything through their preconceptions, ideas based on little or no information, just personal bias. They incorporate their life experience into what they are hearing, making snap interpretations of our every word. They filter everything through their worldview, their knowledge, and understanding.

Then, there is the **association listener**, who evaluates our Christian visit with everything bad they have ever heard of Christianity and the Bible, and we are guilty by association. No matter what we say, it is ignored, because they see us as a member of a group that they perceive a certain way. Of course, this could go the other way if they have a favorable view of Christianity. While these are the negative side of listening, it can give us an idea of why and how we could be shut out, before we ever get started. If we feel that we are unfairly dismissed, we could ask some open-ended questions such as 'how do you feel,' 'what do you think,' 'what do you believe,' or 'how do you see these questions.' Open-ended questions enable us to get to their heart condition, enabling us to formulate our arguments better.

Lastly, there are the persons that all Christian evangelizers are looking for, which is the **receptive heart listener**. One who has a receptive heart will let reasoning from the Scriptures in receptively, which will build confidence in what we are saying is true. We will be able to plant seeds of truth within this person's heart, which God will make grow. In writing to the Corinthians, who were caught up in arguing over who was greater (Paul or Apollos); Paul made the comparison of a Christian evangelist with that of a farmer. The Apostle Paul planted the Corinthian congregation. Apollos came later on the scene and watered the Bible truths that Paul had already planted. Apollos with his passion and force, as well as his authoritative Scriptural refutations of the arguments that had been raised by the unbelieving Jews, was very beneficial to the Corinthian Christians. However, it was God, who made those truths grow.

1 Corinthians 3:1-9 Updated American Standard Version (UASV)

Corinthians Still Fleshly

3 And I, brothers, was not able to speak to you as to spiritual men, but as to fleshly men, as to infants in Christ. ² I gave you milk to drink, not solid food, for you were not yet ready. But now you are still not able, ³ for you are still fleshly. For since there is jealousy and strife among you, are you not fleshly, and are you not walking like mere men? ⁴ For when one says, "I am of Paul," and another, "I am of Apollos," are you not mere men?

God Makes It Grow

⁵ What then is Apollos? And what is Paul? Servants through whom you believed, as the Lord assigned to each. ⁶ I planted, Apollos watered, but God gave the growth. ⁷ So then neither the one who plants nor the one who waters is anything, but only God who gives the growth. ⁸ Now he who plants and he who waters are one; but each will receive his own reward according to his own labor. ⁹ For we are God's fellow workers; you are God's field, God's building.

Keep in mind that the receptive heart listener is not just the person, who shakes his head yes, as he agrees with your every word. Peter was sent to the Ethiopian Eunuch (Acts 8:26-38), who had rapid spiritual progress, while the Apostle Paul was sent to the Greek philosophers on Mars Hill.

Mars Hill (Areopagus) was a "prominent rise overlooking the city of Athens where the philosophers of the city gathered to discuss their ideas, some of which revolutionized modern thought. Paul discussed religion with the leading minds of Athens on Mars Hill. He used the altar to an 'unknown god' to present Jesus to them (Acts 17:22)."[77]

The point is that the Apostle Paul was sent to people who were very knowledgeable, intelligent, and wise, people who only lacked the light to see where the real truth lie. This was no easy assignment, but in the end, "some men joined [Paul] and believed, among whom also were Dionysius the Areopagite and a woman named Damaris and others with them." (Acts 17:34) Yes, Paul reasoned from the Scriptures in the synagogue with the Jews, and he reasoned with Epicurean and Stoic philosophers, who also conversed with him. It says that he was "explaining and proving." This illustrates that a receptive heart listener also includes those who require us to reason from the Scriptures; therefore, we have to have the ability to reason from the Scriptures. (Acts 17: 2-3, 17-18)

Effective Listening and Responding

In trying to communicate with strangers, it can be quite a challenge at times. We may deal with biases, prejudices, a person in the middle of life trauma, someone who has had bad experiences, someone who just lost a loved one, and many more communication challenges. We will be able to overcome some of the anxieties of starting a conversation, by taking a moment to consider some of these challenges.

One of the ways to deal with a challenge is empathy. We in our hearts must place ourselves in their shoes, getting their mindset. Just because a person comes across abrasively about talking about the Bible, this does not mean that we let them go. There may very well be a reason as to why they are not open to a Bible conversation. This is where insightful, thought-provoking questions, can get at the significant part that has closed them down.

By employing active listening, allowing them to vent, we will understand whatever issues we need to overcome. We might ask, 'tell me, what has you to the point where you are unable to talk about the Bible.' This will let them know that we are open to listening. While they are expressing themselves, do not be tempted to resolve their issue, just listen as they fully explain. First, make sure we respond in a calm voice. Then reiterate what they said in a summary point, which will let them know we were listening, and it helps us to know we understand what it is. In the end, we may not agree, but we can empathetically understand in some way.

Now, if we have a solution to what was mention, offer it at this time. If we do not have a biblical answer, be honest, saying something like, "I can understand, and while I do not have a ready answer for you at this time, I will research it at home, and we can talk again." This lets them know that we are going beyond what one would expect and that we are very concerned about them.

---

[77] "Mars Hill", in Holman Illustrated Bible Dictionary, ed. Chad Brand, Charles Draper, Archie England et al., 1084 (Nashville, TN: Holman Bible Publishers, 2003).

REASONING 11 Becoming a Better Communicator

We cannot share in the Great Commission that Jesus assigned every Christian without effectively communicating with others. (Matt. 24:14; 28:19, 20; Acts 1:8) If an intimate family of husband and wife, father and children, mother and children, struggle to communicate with each other, how are we to be expected to communicate well with strangers?

We must empathize with the people whom we are trying to evangelize. Individuals live busy lives, and then they face people trying to sell them things, people trying to get their vote, people trying to debate and argue ideologies, people trying to do them harm, and the list continues. This can force most people to shut out the noise by not talking with strangers. The good thing is we as Christians can communicate a message to strangers even before we say one word. How? We send a nonverbal sign to others just by being different in our appearance, conduct, or behavior. If we were to go to a very big mall [78] and sit watching people for a few hours, would we be able to pick out the Christians in the crowd? Therefore, before we say one word, we communicate by displaying a humble, unassuming personal appearance.

In addition, to communicate effectively, we must not be anxious or appear worried. If we are anxious, then the stranger we approach will be apprehensive. If we display a sense of calm and ease, he will more likely listen to us. What makes us less anxious? The Apostle Peter said that we must **always to be prepared** to make a defense to anyone who asks you for a reason for the hope." (1 Pet. 3:15) Certainly, a well-prepared person is going to be less nervous than someone not prepared. We will draw people to the Good News when they sense this peace of mind that dwells in us.

Communication is a two-way street. If someone tends to dominate a conversation, others will not want to listen to us and may leave. Christ followers need to learn how to be better listeners. If we ask a question, the other person must have their opportunity to speak, not be overcome by one's zeal of sharing our message.[79] Moreover, we must demonstrate evidence that we are listening by looking the other person in the eyes and nodding your head in agreement. You can also ask to clarify questions that dig deeper based on what the person said. Obviously, we go out to talk to others, and we have planned the things that we want to discuss. However, those whom we speak with may have things they want to talk about, so we must be flexible.

One of the most difficult adjustments that must be made is one's attitude. If one views himself as superior in any way, the other person will notice it. Christianity is the truth and the way, but one cannot be dogmatic in his or her expressions.

---

[78] A mall is a large enclosed building complex containing stores, restaurants, and other businesses and facilities serving the general public.

[79] However, people can get off the subject at hand, and begin jumping from one topic to the next. If this proves the case, do not overtake the conversation; just lovingly guide them back on topic.

Moreover, one will talk to liberal Christians,[80] who must be witnessed to just as any unbeliever because they must be led back to the flock. Therefore, suppose one witnesses to a liberal Christian, who is repeatedly making comments that are unbiblical. Correct his unbiblical view, but one ought to not go on a rampage of one correction after another. If this is the first time, one speaks to him, overlook correcting him now. Build a rapport and establish a comfort level by finding common ground if possible. Yes, this may require a measure of self-control, as well as skillful tact. When you meet a second time, choose a topic that you know he raised the first time, and see if you can get him to reason on that one matter. If the other person jumps from subject to subject, it would be best to confine it to one area, but do that with discernment and sensitivity.

Reason With them from the Scriptures

Again, do not sound dogmatic in communicating, but instead, reason with them from the Scriptures, just as Paul did on many occasions. In fact, it says, **"As was his custom,"** meaning that Paul regularly went to the "synagogue of the Jews," to reason with them from the Scriptures, trying to convert them to Christianity. (Acts 17:2, 17; 18:19) To do this, one must be well prepared, which is exactly what any believer must do when one faces liberal or progressive Christians or others who have fallen away because of doubt. (Jude 1:3, 22-23) As one sees much wickedness in the world today, the pain, the suffering, and death have caused many to doubt the very existence of God.[81]

God has tolerated evil, sickness, pain, suffering, and death until today to resolve the issues Satan raises. People become self-centered in thinking that this has only pained us. Imagine that one holds a rope on a sinking ship that 20 other men, women, and children are clinging to when your child loses her grip and falls into the ocean. Either hold the rope, saving 20 people, or let go of the rope and attempt to rescue your child. God has been watching the suffering of billions from the day of Adam's and Eve's sin. Moreover, it has been his great love for us, which causes him to cling to the rope that saves us from a future of the same issues.

Nevertheless, he will not allow this evil to remain forever. He has set a fixed time when he will end this wicked system of Satan's rule. (Eccles. 3:1-8) Galatians 4:4 says, "But when the fullness of time had come, God sent forth his Son, born of woman." However, this was over 4,000 years after he had made the promise to do just that. (Gen. 3:15) Similarly, it has been 2,000 years since God's Word has made the promise to end pain, suffering, and death. When the fullness of time comes, he will do that. One can take the person back to the beginning, and establish that it was man, who willfully entered human beings into this world of imperfection, and the issues raised, offering illustrations why those must be settled first, reasoning from the Scriptures.

---

[80] Christian liberalism is based on a departure from the traditional tenets of biblical Christianity. Often, liberalism within Christian groups begins with a denial of the absolute reliability and historical accuracy of the Word of God. Hindson, Ed (2008-05-01). The Popular Encyclopedia of Apologetics (Kindle Locations 11793-11795). Harvest House Publishers. Kindle Edition.

[81] http://www.christianpublishers.org/suffering-evil-why-god

What It Takes for Effective Communication

Matthew 11:28-30 Updated American Standard Version (UASV)

Jesus' Yoke Is Refreshing

[28] "Come to me, all you who are laboring and loaded down, and I will give you rest. [29] Take my yoke upon you and learn from me, for I am **gentle** and **lowly in heart**, and you will find rest for your souls. [30] For my yoke is easy,[82] and my burden is light."

Yes, if we are going to be an effective communicator, we must learn from Jesus. What do we learn from Jesus? First, Jesus is "gentle," which is the English for the Greek word *praus* that is found "three times in Matthew and once in 1 Peter ... means 'gentle, humble, considerate, meek in the older favorable sense' (BAGD)."[83] In what sense was Jesus, "lowly in heart"?[84] With his knowledge and understanding, as the Son of God, he could have taught in Jewish schools, having some of the greatest Jewish minds as students. He could have taught the Jewish teachers themselves if he so desired.

However, Jesus chose to teach the lowliest of the Jewish world, from the seaside, fishermen. He lived and taught among the poor and the low in social position. It is a privilege to pattern ourselves after such a teacher as he was. This humility and lowliness of heart qualified him as the greatest teacher ever so it will qualify us, as we are taught by him, to be teachers of others. When we are lowly in heart, following in the footsteps of Jesus, we too will refresh others. A teacher who is gentle, humble, considerate, meek, will appeal to both the low and high in social standing. As those with a receptive heart found Jesus refreshing, this will be the case with us as well.

In Acts 20:19, it says that the Apostle Paul served the Lord "with all humility," with "humble-mindedness" or "humility of mind." The Greek (*tapeinophrosune*) literally reads "lowliness of mind."[85] It is derived from the words *tapeinos*, which means to "make low," "lowly, "humble" and *phren*, "the mind." Paul told the Philippians that they were to "do nothing from selfish ambition or conceit, but in humility **["lowliness of mind"]** count others more significant than yourselves." (Phil. 2:3-4) Paul also told the Corinthians, "Let no one seek his own good but the good of the other." (1 Cor. 10:24) This quality of "lowliness of mind" will stop us from assuming a superior attitude or tone when we speak to others about God's Word.

---

[82] I.e. *easy to bear*

[83] Leon Morris, The Gospel According to Matthew, The Pillar New Testament Commentary (Grand Rapids, MI; Leicester, England: W.B. Eerdmans; Inter-Varsity Press, 1992).

[84] The heart ([kardia]) is the core and center of man's being, the mainspring of dispositions as well as of feelings and thoughts. It is the very hub of the wheel of man's existence, the center from which all the spokes radiate (Prov. 4:23; cf. 1 Sam. 16:7). All of this also applies to Christ's human nature.—William Hendriksen and Simon J. Kistemaker, vol. 9, Exposition of the Gospel According to Matthew, New Testament Commentary (Grand Rapids: Baker Book House, 1953-2001).

[85] W. E. Vine, Merrill F. Unger and William White, Jr., vol. 2, Vine's Complete Expository Dictionary of Old and New Testament Words, 314 (Nashville, TN: T. Nelson, 1996).

Additionally, if you want to be effective in your communication, one must follow Paul's counsel found at Colossians 4:6,

Colossians 4:6 Updated American Standard Version (UASV)

⁶ Let your speech always be gracious, seasoned with salt, so that you may know how you ought to answer each person.

Yes, this is the reason that anyone has purchased *The Evangelism Handbook*, to "study how best to talk with each person you meet." Certainly, patience and tact, which is skillfully expressing oneself when another person's feelings are involved, are two qualities that establish effective communication. When one communicates with others, one's words must be in good taste. Good speech will keep lines of communication open, but unwise, foolish, and careless comments will close those lines of communication.

A prepared person will not be anxious but will be relaxed, which will have a calming effect on their listener, too. But allow the listener to do most of the talking, to get at the heart of their thinking. One can never adjust another's thinking because one does not know what is going through their mind. For example, someone could make a comment, and one could choose a phrase and give several minutes of feedback, which proves to be irrelevant to what the person meant. It would have been better to ask, "What do you mean by …?" Once the person explains themselves, then we can offer our thoughts.

Loving Communication

The characteristics of being gentle, humble, considerate, meek, modest, lowliness of mind, tactfulness and patience make the qualities of a good communicator. When a person also has selfless love, he or she becomes a great communicator.

Matthew 9:36 Updated American Standard Version (UASV)

³⁶ When he saw the crowds, he had compassion for them, because they were **harassed** and **scattered**, like sheep without a shepherd.

Mark 6:34 Updated American Standard Version (UASV)

³⁴ When he went ashore he saw a great crowd, and he had compassion on them, because they were like sheep without a shepherd. And he began to teach them many things.

"**Harassed** is from a verb meaning to trouble, distress. **Scattered** is from a verb meaning to throw down. The past tense used here implies the thoroughness of their oppression and its persistent effect on the people. These people were completely and perpetually discouraged."[86] The Jewish religious leaders of Jesus' day did next to nothing in offering enough to make common people feel pleased or content in their spiritual hunger. Rather, they made their lives even more burdensome with all of their rules and regulations that they tacked on to the Mosaic Law. (Matt. 12:1, 2; 15:1-9; 23:4, 23) The religious leaders revealed their true heart condition when they said about those listening to Jesus, "this crowd who does not know the law is

---

[86] Stuart K. Weber, vol. 1, Matthew, Holman New Testament Commentary, 130 (Nashville, TN: Broadman & Holman Publishers, 2000).

accursed!" (John 7:49) Jesus' selfless love moved him to "find rest for their souls," getting on the road to life. Today, we have a message that is filled with love as well, and believers must offer love to people in a selfless way, too.

1 Thessalonians 2:7-8 Updated American Standard Version (UASV)

[7] But we became gentle[87] in the midst of you, as a nursing mother tenderly care for[88] her own children. [8] So, being affectionately desirous of you, we were well-pleased to impart to you not only the gospel of God but also our own souls,[89] because you became beloved to us.

2:7. Instead, Paul and Silas chose to be **gentle**. There is no tenderness quite like a mother's, and Paul dared to identify with maternal love and care. Greek writers used the term *gentleness* to describe those who dealt patiently and with a mild manner toward those who were difficult—obstinate children, unmanageable students, those who had not reached maturity and were experiencing the inconsistencies and struggles of development. Whatever difficulties the Thessalonians may have presented, Paul and Silas recognized that these new Christians were not yet "grown up." So rather than dealing with these people in an authoritarian manner, they chose to be patient—like a mother.

It is a great lesson for the church today, because we have not always been patient with new or young believers. Sometimes we have cut a mold and demanded that they fit it—now. Instead of this approach, we need to see each individual's need for help and encouragement as he or she struggles to conform to the image of Christ.

2:8. Here is a classic understanding of biblical love. To Paul, love is always a verb, it is doing. Feelings may accompany love, but they do not define it. Instead, the commitment of acting in the best interest of another opens the way for feelings: **We loved you so much that we were delighted to share ... our lives.**

It is easier to teach theology than to love, easier to share lists than time. Paul gave not only the message of the gospel, but the example of it as well. He spent time. He shared joys and headaches. Parents and teachers, coaches and mentors, pastors and leaders know what it means to give part of their heart away to others. Love is not just a job. It is a way of life.

But note that Paul did *share* the gospel of God. He was balanced. He gave his life and love. He gave content as well. It is not enough to visit people in the hospital or prison, or to show compassion to the poor or those new in the faith. Somewhere, carefully and candidly, they must also hear the truth of the cross and what it means to trust and follow Christ.

Arguing whether the church should meet people's physical needs or whether it should limit itself to preaching the gospel is like debating which wing of an airplane is more important. Both are essential![90]

---

[87] Some MSS read *babes*

[88] Or *cherishes*

[89] Or *lives*

[90] Knute Larson, *I & II Thessalonians, I & II Timothy, Titus, Philemon*, vol. 9, Holman New Testament Commentary (Nashville, TN: Broadman & Holman Publishers, 2000), 23–24.

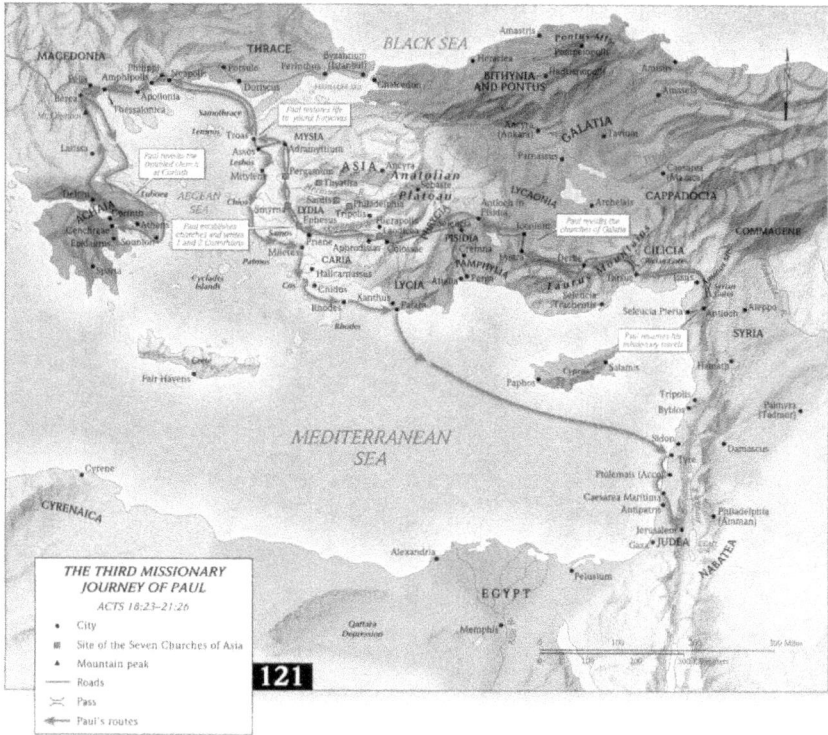

THE THIRD MISSIONARY
JOURNEY OF PAUL
ACTS 18:23–21:26

• City
■ Site of the Seven Churches of Asia
▲ Mountain peak
— Roads
⊃⊂ Pass
←— Paul's routes

The Apostle Paul started numerous congregations, one right after the other, from Antioch of Syria, throughout Asia, into Macedonia, down through Greece and Achaia. What made Paul such an effective evangelist? Was it his zeal for spreading the Good News? Yes! The above says that Paul was **"affectionately desirous"** of the new Thessalonian congregation. "Here is a classic understanding of biblical love. To Paul, love is always a verb; it is doing. Feelings may accompany love, but they do not define it. Instead, the commitment to acting in the best interest of another opens the way for feelings: **We loved you so much that we were delighted to share ... our lives.**"[91] The love Paul had for God, and his neighbor made him a successful evangelist.

If our message is repeatedly rejected, is this a sign of poor communication skills? It could be, but keep in mind; most are going to reject the Christian message. The majority of the world will not be converted to true Christianity by the time of Christ's second coming. In addition, when we consider Christianity as a whole, most are false. We are only after a select few, which are actually many when we consider there are seven billion in the world. Believers must be in search for those that are open and true, modest, and seeking. Have you done your best to be an effective communicator of God's Word, when any opportunity presents itself? If you

---

[91] Knute Larson, vol. 9, I & II Thessalonians, I & II Timothy, Titus, Philemon, Holman New Testament Commentary, 24 (Nashville, TN: Broadman & Holman Publishers, 2000).

answered yes, and people still have rejected the message, they are not rejecting you, but they are rejecting God. If you answered no, then there is work to do.

REASONING 12 Active Listening to Fully Understand

Luke 8:18 Updated American Standard Version (UASV)

[18] Therefore, take care how you listen; for whoever has, to him more shall be given; and whoever does not have, even what he thinks he has shall be taken away from him."

Jesus' caution to his audience about how they listen proves just as relevant today as it was 2,000 years ago. If one only hears the words, but not what lies behind those words, he will find himself in trouble with his spouse, children, employer, and everyone else he communicates with daily. More importantly, it could jeopardize one's hope of eternal life. We need to consider more than the words themselves.

We must hear the words that are spoken, as well as the way it is said, the tone and the body language, to get the sense of what someone means. A common complaint of wives to husbands is that they passively listen to them, blocking out much of what they do not want to hear, because they oppose, or are not interested in what she is saying. Sadly, we tend to be less appreciative of those who are closest to us than total strangers. Active listening is a form of listening that results in the speaker and listener having a full understanding of what is meant. There are seven points to active listening:

(1) **Pay close attention** to what is being said; listen for the ideas behind the words. Do not just hear, but also feel the words. Let the speaker know that you are listening, by leaning forward a little, looking at him, not staring, but having sufficient eye contact.

(2) **Look at** the facial expression, the tone of the voice, the inflection of the voice, the mood and body language. Get at the feelings behind the words. People generally do not say all that is on their mind or convey their true feelings at times, so the listener must pay close attention to the non-verbal signs.

(3) **Turn off your internal thinking** as much as possible. In other words, do not be thinking of how to respond to certain points while he is still talking, because you are going to miss the whole of what he has said.

(4) Let the speaker know you are paying attention by **nodding from time to time**, as well as acknowledging with verbal gestures.

(5) **Reiterate** is not a common word, but it means to repeat what you think the person meant by what they said, but in your own words, to see if you understood them correctly. "So, you mean ... right?"

(6) The person you are speaking with will acknowledge that you are correct, or he will correct you and will restate what they meant, and likely in a more comprehensive way since you misunderstood. **Pay even closer attention** as they explain again, what they meant.

(7) When they have explained their message again, you must **repeat your reiteration.**

Considering how to listen proves vital if we are going to be an effective evangelizer. There has been no greater teacher than Jesus Christ because he was an effective communicator, as well as an active listener. While some may be effective speakers, very motivational and moving, they lack teaching skills. Every time we open our mouths to share the Good News with another person, be it five minutes, or an ongoing study with them, we must build a relationship with them.

Jesus in the Temple at Twelve Years Old

Luke 2:41-47 Updated American Standard Version (UASV)

[41] Now his parents went to Jerusalem every year at the Feast of the Passover. [42] And when he was twelve years old, they went up according to the custom of the feast. [43] And after the days were completed, while they were returning, the boy Jesus stayed behind in Jerusalem. And his parents did not know it, [44] but supposing him to be in the company, they went a day's journey; and they began looking for him among their relatives and acquaintances. [45] and when they did not find him, they returned to Jerusalem, looking for him. [46] Then, it occurred, after three days they found him in the temple, sitting in the midst of the teachers and listening to them and questioning them. [47] And all those listening to him were amazed at his understanding and his answers.

This incident develops into something far more magnificent than one might first realize. Kittel's *Theological Dictionary of the New Testament* helps the reader appreciate that the Greek word *eperotao*, which means to ask, to question, to demand of, for "questioning" was far more than the Greek word *erotao* to ask, to request, to entreat, for a boy's inquisitiveness. *Eperotao* can refer to questioning, which one might hear in a judicial hearing, such as a scrutiny, inquiry, counter questioning, even the "probing and cunning questions of the Pharisees and Sadducees," for instance those we find in Mark 10:2 and 12:18-23.

The same dictionary continues: "In [the] face of this usage it may be asked whether ... [Luke] 2:46 denotes, not so much the questioning curiosity of the boy, but rather His successful disputing. [Verse] 47 would fit in well with the latter view." Rotherham's translation of verse 47 presents it as a dramatic confrontation: "Now all who heard him were beside themselves, because of his understanding and his answers." Robertson's Word Pictures in the New Testament says that their constant amazement means, "They stood out of themselves as if their eyes were bulging out."

After returning to Jerusalem, and three days of searching, they found young Jesus in the Temple, questioning the Jewish religious leaders, to which "they were astounded." (Luke 2:48) Robertson said of this, "(The) second aorist passive indicative of an old Greek word [*ekplesso*]), to strike out, drive out by a blow. Joseph and Mary 'were struck out' by what they saw and heard. Even they had not fully realized the power in this wonderful boy."[92] Thus, at twelve years old, Jesus,

---

[92] A.T. Robertson, Word Pictures in the New Testament (Nashville, TN: Broadman Press, 1933), Lk 2:48.

but a boy, is already demonstrating he is a great teacher and defender of truth. BDAG says, "To cause to be filled with amazement to the point of being overwhelmed, amaze, astound, overwhelm (lit., strike out of one's senses)."[93]

The Jewish culture, and especially Jesus' Jewish family, displayed an effective ability to listen. The Jewish religious leaders, on the other hand, seemed eager to speak, not listen. Jesus was not in the temple to win conversations with the greatest teachers of Jewish Law, but rather to listen. It says in verse 46 that the twelve-year-old Jesus was "listening to them." Once he listened to them, he then knew what they meant, their motives for what they said, and it was at that time, he proceeded in **"asking them questions."** Good listening leads to good questions.

Verse 47 says, "All who heard him were amazed at his insight and his answers," which means that Jesus' questions were intensely insightful, and even penetrating. If one finds himself in a conversation with a Bible critic in a public setting, where others are listening, we must listen. If one discerns that the Bible critic does not have a receptive heart, and nothing we say will open his eyes to the truth of God's Word, we must consider others who may be listening. Because of that larger audience, one will then do as Jesus did, use effective questions to put the Bible critic on defense, so that those around know we do have answers for the criticisms, giving them faith in the message they heard.

Do Not Allow Yourself to Get in the Way

Passive involvement in a discussion can lead to getting in the way of our own objective. One must be aware that not everyone has taken the time to read a book on effective communication. Therefore, a person in the conversation may be someone who goes on for some time and gets lost or sidetracked with other subjects not relevant to the discussion. If that occurs, respectfully stop them, and briefly explain that it would be best to stay on topic, and offer that person the point that they were making.

Overzealousness also proves another way that we get in the way of our own objective. A trap that one can fall into with a very active mind is anticipating what the speaker will say. It can be rude to interrupt them by finishing their thoughts, or worse, to assume what they will say, and then offer feedback on one's assumption. Many times that leads to the response, "I was not going to say that at all, what I was going to say was ...." Each time one interrupts the other speaker *unnecessarily*, that person withdraws further and further from being an active participant in the conversation. Rather, let the person finish their thoughts, and hold off for a few seconds to see if they will start again before you respond.

The person, who may seem like a Bible critic, can make a believer defensive, which can unnerve most evangelists. If someone approaches a believer with an alleged error or contradiction, what should we do? We should be frank and honest. If we do not have an answer, we should admit such. If the text in question gives

---

[93] William Arndt, Frederick W. Danker and Walter Bauer, A Greek-English Lexicon of the New Testament and Other Early Christian Literature, 3rd ed. (Chicago: University of Chicago Press, 2000), 308.

111

the appearance of difficulty, we should admit this as well. If a believer remains unsure how to answer, simply say that you will look into it and get back to them, returning with a reasonable answer.

However, do not express disbelief and doubt to people who have legitimate concerns about the Bible, because they will be moved even further in their disbelief. Moreover, it will put them on offense and place the believer on defense. With great confidence, tell them there is an answer. The Bible has withstood the test of 2,000 years of persecution and is the most printed book of all time, currently being translated into 2,287 languages. If these critical questions threatened its credibility, the Bible would not be the book that it is.

The evangelist must keep Paul's words "knowledge puffs up" at the fore of his thinking because as one grows in knowledge and understanding, it is too easy to fall prey to a haughty spirit. After the evangelist has spent hundreds of hours listening to unbelievers talk about the Bible, one will hear the same thing many times. This is like watching the same uninteresting movie dozens of times. This can cause the evangelist to start speaking in a disdainful tone to the person who is speaking. It may be blatant, or even subtle, but the unbeliever will notice it, and while they may respectfully finish the conversation with the evangelist, they will not care what the believer said before the end of the conversation.

Proverbs 16:18 Updated American Standard Version (UASV)

18 Pride goes before destruction,
and a haughty spirit before a fall.

In the end, God has given each of us the right to make our own decisions. The evangelist that respects another person's right to their views may win the day in the end. If a Bible critic goes through a conversation with both speakers having an equal time, they will feel that they were respected. They will be open to speaking to another Christian at another time. We must keep in mind that we are planting seeds of truth. Life experiences have a way of altering heart conditions. One unbeliever may have something happen in their life, which makes them more receptive to Bible truths, and the next Christian they engage will have success in watering those seeds.

Getting Beneath the Surface

In witnessing to others, there will come times when one feels the other person is holding back. The unbeliever really does not want to go deeper into the conversation because perhaps she does not want to offend. Maybe she views the Bible or God as foolish, and anyone that holds them as truth, just as foolish. Therefore, they just give surface answers to finish the conversation. Gently and respectfully ask some questions that will probe beneath the surface answers that she has been supplying. One could ask, "Can you tell me more about ...? What is it that has brought you to this conclusion?"

In some cases, people hold back because of past hurts. Maybe their child died, and this has only reinforced to them that there cannot be a loving God. They may not feel like sharing the hurt, so he attempts to get out of the conversation. If a couple of tactful questions might get them to open up, go ahead. However, if it seems that additional questions will do more damage than good, let it go because they will respect the believer for handling the conservation that way. On the other hand, if the searching questions prove effective, and the person becomes emotional in explaining why they have not been able to accept God, do not get analytical; rather, be a comforter who is an empathetic and understanding listener.

How questions are asked can make all the difference. If one seeks answers that lie beneath the surface, we should avoid the "why" questions, because they come across in more like an interrogation. This may make the other person close down even further. You can use qualifiers to get deeper. Thus, it would not be, "Why do you not believe in God?" Rather it would be, "What has contributed to your understanding of God?" Another way might be to ask, "How have you have come to your current position on God?" Searching questions at the right time come about because a believer has been an active listener.

REASONING 13 Look for Opportunities to Establish Rapport

Rapport is pronounced ra•páwr, as the "t" is silent. The *Encarta Dictionary* defines rapport as "an emotional bond or friendly relationship between people based on mutual liking, trust, and a sense that they understand and share each other's concerns." There likely have been times when you connected with someone the first time you met him or her. It seemed as though you were of the same mind, the same line of thought. Some synonyms to rapport are "understanding, bond, link, affinity, fellow feeling, connection, empathy, camaraderie, affiliation, and fellowship." People need this bond is in every walk of life. It proves especially important in the family, with your friends, in the church, in the workplace, and with any new connections. This ability to build rapport or to bond with others is paramount in the work of an evangelist.

Rapport in the Life of the Evangelist

One must establish a genuine connection with those that whom you witness to; otherwise, they will notice the lack of sincerity. Everyone loves to share their thoughts on this, which means open-ended questions are the best way to get the conversation moving. As a believer begins a conversation, invite them to express themselves, and take note of their home, if that is where you are talking with them. Do they have pets? Has something just been remolded? Do they have children? Are there things sitting out that show a university someone attended? The objective is to get to know the person to whom you are witnessing by showing interest in them. The believer must have some idea of what that person believes, which will build an even stronger bond. Perhaps the believer takes notice that she is wearing a cross, but is she Catholic or Protestant? What denomination is she a part of, and how often does she attend? Bring these observations to the surface; however, the believer must be willing to share some of their life. There must be a balance because you do not want to leave the unbeliever feeling they have been interrogated.

Current Affairs

Once a believer has done that, ask a question about some troubling current event. This will let one know their beliefs and values as they address your questions. If you are at their home and they have magazines lying around, which show they follow world events, you might ask: "Have you been following the unrest in the Middle East? If it does not appear that they follow world events; think of something local. It should be within their state or a neighboring state, but that has made national news, such as the George Zimmerman trial in the death of Trayvon Martin. These insights that one gain will determine if they are conservative or liberal. It is important to remember that how one asks a question is just as important as what is asked. Try to be neutral in the question, not giving away how you may feel about the current affair because the believer wants their true assessment.

Scriptural Beliefs

Answers to these questions help a believer know how to move the discussion into more of a biblical conversation. Starting with the Bible may compel the listener to say, "I do not discuss religion." Because one has gained the trust of the listener, he or she will feel more comfortable talking about the Bible. When a believer engages a person, be prepared not to judge them on their views. Facial expressions and body language will give away feelings. If an unbeliever has issues with Christianity, religion, or even certain segments of Christianity, there may be genuine reasons why the person has those views. Maybe the person believes the Bible is just a book by men. Maybe he or she dislikes the hypocrisy of religion. Maybe the only Christianity the person knows is the televangelists they catch on television.

Whatever the unbeliever displays, be empathetic to their circumstances. However, this also is the time to share a couple of Scriptural thoughts, which will differ based on what has been learned about him. However, share some texts that demonstrate understanding and let your loving kindness and tact shine through at this time. (Gal. 5:22; 2 Cor. 6:3, 4, 6) Get these interested ones to open up to gain a sense of whom they are, and then use a couple of applicable texts in the conversation, leaving an opening to visit with them again.

Open-Ended Questions

Open-ended questions allow an answer that is more than a simple yes or no. These usually include: "Whom would you say …?"; "What do you think …?"; "Where did you …?"; "Why do you think …?"; "How did you …?" or "Tell me more about …." These questions or statements open things up, enabling the believer to discover their worldview. You may ask, "Do you think all of this hideous violence in the world suggests that something more than man has a role in these events?" This may just result in a simple yes or no. One could also ask, "With everyone wanting happiness, yet there is so much evil in the world, why do you think that is the case?"

Ask questions that generate a sense of an invitation, not pressure. One could ask, "What do you believe will bring about world peace?" Once the person gives their response, push on with, "What makes you feel that way?" In street witnessing, one could ask those with children, "What do you think life will be like for them when they are adults?" Then follow with, "What is it that concerns you the most about their future?" None of these questions should make the listener feel uncomfortable.

Draw It Out

Proverbs 20:5 Updated American Standard Version (UASV)

⁵ Counsel in a man's heart is like deep water,
   but a man of understanding draws it out.

Everyone is different. The melting pot[94] of races, cultures, and worldviews has seen an explosion over the last 30 years and seems far removed from the Christian community by way of language, customs, and lifestyle. You may live in a community that has numerous cultures. So, be prepared to adjust the approach to suit the person and circumstances, such as topic and tone. How does one draw people out? This is done by allowing them to speak while you serve as the guide of the conversation, merely keeping the other person on the subject, or involve them in numerous topics. If one wants a deep discussion on just one topic, let the other person speak, but make sure they stay on topic. Their thoughts must be appreciated, so attach the appropriate facial expression and body language to what the other person says, with comments such as "interesting," true," "I never thought of it that way," and so on. Acknowledge every time both of you are on common ground: "Yes, I feel that way too." To interject a Scripture, one could add, "You know the Bible touches on that. Let me share the verse ..." Most importantly, never water down Bible truth, but do not be unbending or confrontational.

Success in generating rapport depends on *listening skills.* An Unbeliever will be able to sense if one's heart is in the conversation. By giving that person space and time to unload their thoughts, react to them from the heart. This will serve as another point of attraction. Showing another person respect and honor, by active listening, they will be more likely to listen to biblical truths shared with them.

Making Contact

There are certain gestures that will contribute to others being attracted to your biblical message. We have discussed active listening at length, but there is also physical contact, eye contact, and expressing deep respect in our voice and body language. You must be very cautious when touching others, but laying your hand on their shoulder a couple times in a conversation, can truly make some feel your warmth toward them. Shaking their hand is also an appropriate gesture. Women should not touch men, and men should not touch women. If a woman touches a man, this may send the wrong signal. If a man touches a woman, this may startle her, pushing her away, not drawing her in. We return to the cultures as well, because some Asians do not like to be touched, as is true of some Jewish cultures as well.

Learning to Listen

As discussed above, the more one uncovers about the person to whom you witness to, the greater the bond that will form. To learn more, one must listen to the way the person acts and reacts in the conversation. But we know that humans typically do not listen well. Wives can attest to this based on their husband's selective listening habits. However, listening can be improved. Not only does one want to hear the words of the other person, but what do he mean by the words he used. This would include noticing what he does not say as much as what he says.

---

[94] A melting pot is "a place where a variety of races, cultures, or individuals assimilate into a cohesive whole.—Inc Merriam-Webster, Merriam-Webster's Collegiate Dictionary., Eleventh ed. (Springfield, MA: Merriam-Webster, Inc., 2003).

Guiding the Conversation

Either a believer can allow a conversation to branch off and flow in whatever natural direction it takes you, or one can guide the conversation in the intended direction. The first time one speaks with someone about God's Word, choose the former over the latter because the believer collects an understanding of the other person: a Protestant, a Catholic, an atheist, an agnostic, a person who follows Eastern religions, a conservative, a liberal, or somewhere in between. Once you understand the other person, you may wish to move to guiding the conversation's direction.

To build the bond with the listener, stay at the pace of the listener's behavior and body language. By this, one will gain their trust and attention. They will begin to trust the believer, and naturally, allow him or her to lead in the conversation. The same pace simply means the believer reflects the person who listens. This means that if they stand or sit casually, the believer stands or sits casually. If they are serious in conversation, the believer displays seriousness in conversation. If they exhibit light-heartedness, the believer becomes light-hearted. If they act warm and friendly, the believer returns warmth and friendliness, which should happen at all times. If they act lively and energetic, the believer becomes lively and energetic. However, if they become agitated, the believer would not reflect that. Witnessing cannot be the childhood game of mocking the other person, by repeating what he says or does. Develop a natural bond with one another.

In order to appreciate why you are pacing the listener, we might think of the Old West, and the cowboy and the cow.[95] The cowboy is skilled at keeping pace with the cow, to guide it where the cowboy wants the cow to go. When the cow goes where it wants, the horse moves him where the cowboy directs. If the cow horse does not keep pace, but instead falls behind, or gets ahead, he can never take the lead and guide the cow.[96] Once the believer comfortably matches the listener, begin guiding him or her. In this, you set the pace and direction. However, do not rush because the transition in being the guide must be taken slowly.

---

[95] http://www.youtube.com/watch?v=yIBo8E3UXMw
[96] IBID

REASONING

FROM THE SCRIPTURES

Sharing CHRIST as You Help Others to Learn about the Mighty Works of God

HOLY BIBLE

EDWARD D. ANDREWS

CHRISTIAN
APOLOGETIC EVANGELISM

REACHING HEARTS WITH THE ART OF PERSUASION

All Christians Are Scripturally Obligated to Evangelize—Matt. 24:14; 28:19-20; Ac 1:8

EDWARD D. ANDREWS

SECOND EDITION

CONVERSATIONAL EVANGELISM

Defending the Faith, Reasoning from the
Scriptures, Explaining and Proving,
Instructing in Sound Doctrine, and
Overturning False Reasoning

Edward D. Andrews

SECOND EDITION

THE CHRISTIAN APOLOGIST

Always Being Prepared to Make a Defense

Andrews provides an excellent apologetic tool for Christians seeking to better understand & defend the Word of God."—Christian Publishing House

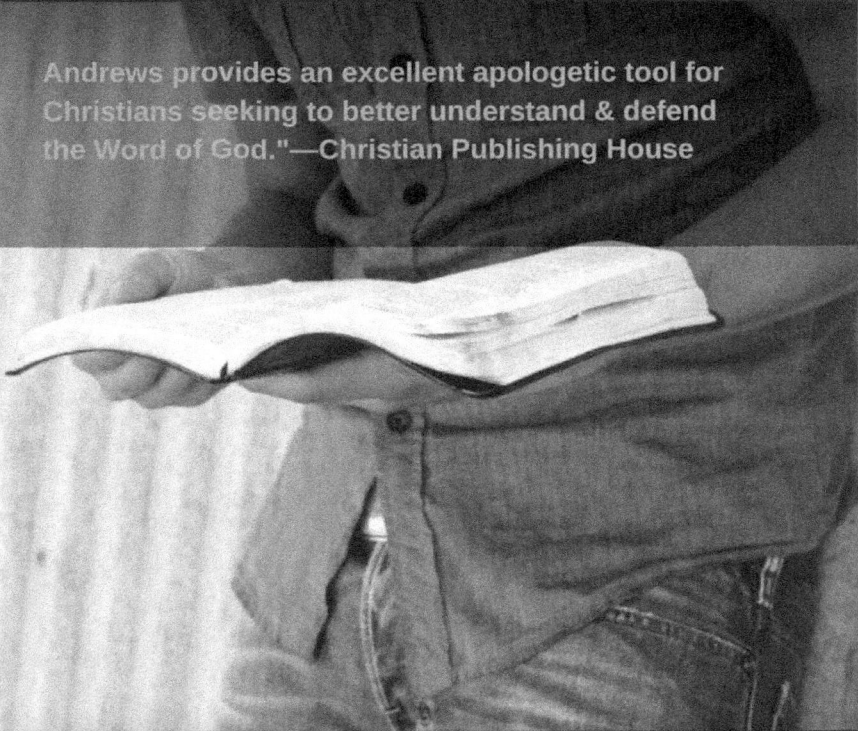

EDWARD D. ANDREWS

SECOND EDITION

THE EVANGELISM HANDBOOK

How All Christians Can Effectively Share God's Word in Their Community

Matthew 9:37-38: Then he said to his disciples, "The harvest is plentiful, but the laborers are few. Therefore beg the Master of the harvest to send out workers into his harvest."

Matthew 24:14; 28:18-20: Jesus said, "this gospel of the kingdom will be proclaimed in all the inhabited earth." "... Go therefore and make disciples of all nations ... teaching them ..."

Edward D. Andrews

THE
APOSTLE PAUL

WHAT MADE THE APOSTLE PAUL'S TEACHING,
PREACHING, EVANGELISM, AND APOLOGETICS
OUTSTANDINGLY EFFECTIVE?

KENNY RHODES, TERRY OVERTON,
& EDWARD D. ANDREWS

HOW TO STUDY YOUR BIBLE

Rightly Handling the Word of God

Edward D. Andrews

Bibliography

Akin, Daniel L. *The New American Commentary: 1, 2, 3 John.* Nashville, TN: Broadman & Holman, 2001.

Aldrich, C Joseph. *Lifestyle Evangelism* XE **"Evangelism"** \b . Portland, OR: Multnoma Press, 1981.

Anders, Max. *Holman New Testament Commentary: vol. 8, Galatians, Ephesians, Philippians, Colossians.* Nashville, TN: Broadman & Holman Publishers, 1999.

—. *Holman Old Testament Commentary - Proverbs* . Nashville: B&H Publishing, 2005.

Anders, Max, and Doug McIntosh. *Holman Old Testament Commentary - Deuteronomy.* Nashville: B&H Publishing, 2009.

Anders, Max, and Steven Lawson. *Holman Old Testament Commentary - Psalms: 11.* Grand Rapids: B&H Publishing, 2004.

Anders, Max, and Trent Butler. *Holman Old Testament Commentary: Isaiah.* Nashiville, TN: B&H Publishing, 2002.

Andrews, Edward D. *THE EVANGELISM HANDBOOK: How All Christians Can Effectively Share God's Word in Their Community.* Cambridge: Christian Publishing House, 2013.

Andrews, Edward D. *THE CHRISTIAN APOLOGIST: Always Being Prepared to Make a Defense* . Cambridge: Christian Publishing House, 2014.

Andrews, Stephen J, and Robert D Bergen. *Holman Old Testament Commentary: 1-2 Samuel.* Nashville: Broadman & Holman, 2009.

Bercot, David W. *A Dictionary of Early Christian Beliefs.* Peabody: Hendrickson, 1998.

Boa, Kenneth, and William Kruidenier. *Holman New Testament Commentary: Romans.* Nashville: Broadman & Holman, 2000.

Brand, Chad, Charles Draper, and England Archie. *Holman Illustrated Bible Dictionary: Revised, Updated and Expanded.* Nashville, TN: Holman, 2003.

Bromiley, Geoffrey W., and Gerhard Friedrich. *Theological Dictionary of the New Testament, ed. Gerhard Kittel, vol. 4.* Grand Rapids, MI: Eerdmans, 1964-.

Brooks, Ronald M, and Norman L Geisler. *Come, Let Us Reason: An Introduction to Logical Thinking.* Grand Rapids: Baker Books, 1990.

Butler, Trent C. *Holman New Testament Commentary: Luke.* Nashville, TN: Broadman & Holman Publishers, 2000.

Butler, Trent C. *Holman Old Testament Commentary - Hosea, Joel, Amos, Obadiah, Jonah, Micah .* Nashville: Broadman & Holman Publishers, 2005.

Carpenter, Eugene E., and Philip W Comfort. *The Holman Treasury of Key Bible Words: 200 Greek and 200 Hebrew Words Defined and Explained.* Nashville: Broadman & Holman Publishers, 2000.

Carson, D. A. *New Bible Commentary: 21st Century Edition. 4th ed.* Downers Grove: Inter-Varisity Press, 1994.

Coleman, E. Robert. *The Master Plan of Evangelism* XE "**Evangelism**" \b . Westwood, NJ: Fleming H. Revell Company, 1964.

Cooper, Rodney. *Holman New Testament Commentary: Mark.* Nashville: Broadman & Holman Publishers, 2000.

Craig, William Lane. *On Guard: Defending Your Faith with Reason and Precision.* Ontario: David C. Cook, 2010.

Dockery, David S. *HOLMAN CONCISE BIBLE COMMENTARY Simple, straightforward commentary on every book of the Bible.* Nashville: Broadman & Holman, 1998.

Easley, Kendell H. *Holman New Testament Commentary, vol. 12, Revelation.* (Nashville, TN: Broadman & Holman Publishers, 1998.

Easton, M. G. *Easton's Bible Dictionary.* Oak Harbor, WA: Logos Research Systems, 1996, c1897.

Edwards, James R. *The Pillar New Testament Commentary: The Gospel according to Mark.* Grand Rapids: Wm. B. Eerdmans Publishing Co., 2002.

Eims, LeRoy. *One to One Evangelism* XE "**Evangelism**" \b . Wheaton, IL: Victor Books, 1974, 1990.

Elwell, Walter A. *Baker Encyclopedia of the Bible.* Grand Rapids: Baker Book House, 1988.

—. *Evangelical Dictionary of Theology (Second Edition).* Grand Rapids: Baker Academic, 2001.

Elwell, Walter A, and Philip Wesley Comfort. *Tyndale Bible Dictionary.* Wheaton, Ill: Tyndale House Publishers, 2001.

Freedman, David Noel, Allen C. Myers, and Astrid B. Beck. *Eerdmans Dictionary of the Bible .* Grand Rapids, Mich.: W.B. Eerdmans , 2000.

Gangel, Kenneth O. *Holman New Testament Commentary: Acts.* Nashville, TN: Broadman & Holman Publishers, 1998.

Gangel, Kenneth O. *Holman New Testament Commentary, vol. 4, John* . Nashville, TN: Broadman & Holman Publishers, 2000.

—. *Holman Old Testament Commentary: Daniel.* Nashville: Broadman & Holman Publishers, 2001.

Geisler, Norman, and David Geisler. *CONVERSATION EVANGELISM: How to Listen and Speak So You Can Be Heard.* Eugene: Harvest House Publishers, 2014.

Green, Joel B, Scot McKnight, and Howard Marshall. *Dictionary of Jesus and the Gospels.* Downers Grove, IL: InterVarsity Press, 1992.

Guder, Darrell L. *Missional Church: A Vision for the Sending of the Church in North America.* Grand Rapids: Wm. B Eerdmans Publishing Co., 1998.

Hastings, James, John A Selbie, and John C Lambert. *A Dictionary of Christ and the Gospels.* New York, NY: Charles Scribner's Sons, 1907.

Hindson, Ed, and Ergun Caner. *The Popular Encyclopedia of Apologetics: Surveying the Evidence for the Truth of Christianity.* Eugene: Harvest House, 2008.

Kennedy, D. James. *Evangelism* XE **"Evangelism"** \b *Explosion.* Wheaton, IL: Tyndale House Publishers, 1977.

Kistemaker, Simon J., and William Hendriksen. *Exposition of the First Epistle to the Corinthians, vol. 18, New Testament Commentary.* Grand Rapids, MI: Baker Book House, 1953–2001.

Knight, George W. *The Pastoral Epistles: A Commentary on the Greek Text, New International Greek Testament Commentary.* Grand Rapids, MI; Carlisle, England: W.B. Eerdmans; Paternoster Press, 1992.

Larsen, L. David. *The Evangelism* XE **"Evangelism"** \b *Mandate.* Wheaton: Crossway Books, 1992.

Larson, Knute. *Holman New Testament Commentary, vol. 9, I & II Thessalonians, I & II Timothy, Titus, Philemon.* Nashville, TN: Broadman & Holman Publishers, 2000.

Lea, Thomas D. *Holman New Testament Commentary: Vol. 10, Hebrews, James.* Nashville, TN: Broadman & Holman Publishers, 1999.

Lea, Thomas D., and Hayne P. Griffin. *The New American Commentary, vol. 34, 1, 2 Timothy, Titus.* Nashville: Broadman & Holman Publishers, 1992.

Louw, Johannes P, Eugene A Nida, Smith. Rondal B, and Karen A Munson. *GREEK-ENGLISH NEW TESTAMENT Based on Semantic Domains (Vol. 1, Second Edition).* New York: United Bible Societies, 1988, 1989.

Manser, Martin H. (Managing Editor) McGrath, Alister E. (General Editor) Packer, J. I. (Consultant Editor). *DICTIONARY OF BIBLE THEMES: The Accessible and Comprehenssive Tool for Topical Studies.* Grand Rapids: Zondervan Publishing Company, 2009.

Martin, Glen S. *Holman Old Testament Commentary: Numbers.* Nashville: Broadman & Holman Publishers, 2002.

Mayers, Mark K. *Christianity Confronts Culture: A Strategy for Crosscultural Evangelism* XE "**Evangelism**" \b . Grand Rapids: Zondervan, 1987.

McCue, Rolland. *Promises Unfulfilled: The Failed Strategy of Modern Evangelism* XE "**Evangelism**" \b . Greenville, SC: Ambassador Group, 2004.

McRaney, William. *The Art of Personal Evangelism* XE "**Evangelism**" \b . Nashville: Broadman & Holman, 2003.

Mirriam-Webster, Inc. *Mirriam-Webster's Collegiate Dictionary. Eleventh Edition.* Springfield: Mirriam-Webster, Inc., 2003.

Mitchell, Michael R. "The Conditions of Discipleship." *Liberty University.* 2004. http://bb7.liberty.edu/webapps/portal/frameset.jsp?tab_tab_group_id=_2_1&url=%2Fwebapps%2Fblackboard%2Fexecute%2Flauncher%3Ftype%3DCourse%26id%3D_998944_ (accessed September 29, 2010).

Mitchell, Michael R. *Leading, Teaching, and Making Disciples: World-Class Education in the Church, School, and Home.* Bloomington: Crossbooks, 2010.

Morgenthaler, Sally. *Worship Evangelism* XE "**Evangelism**" \b . Grand Rapids: Zondervan Publishing House, 1995.

Mounce, William D. *Mounce's Complete Expository Dictionary of Old & New Testament Words.* Grand Rapids, MI: Zondervan, 2006.

Myers, Allen C. *The Eerdmans Bible Dictionary* . Grand Rapids, Mich: Eerdmans, 1987.

Nash, Ronald H. *Life's Ultimate Questions: An Introduction to Philosophy.* Grand Rapids, MI: Zondervan, 1999.

Packer, J. I. *Evangelism* XE "**Evangelism**" \b *and the Sovereignty of God.* Downers Grove, IL: InterVarsity Press, 1979.

Posterski, C. Donald. *Reinventing Evangelism* XE **"Evangelism"** \b . Downers Grove, IL: InterVarsity Press, 1989.

Pratt Jr, Richard L. *Holman New Testament Commentary: I & II Corinthians, vol. 7.* Nashville: Broadman & Holman Publishers, 2000.

Rainer, S. Thomas. *Evangelism* XE **"Evangelism"** \b *in the Twenty-First Century.* Wheaton, IL: Harold Shaw Publishers, 1989.

Reid, Alvin. *Introduction to Evangelism* XE **"Evangelism"** \b . Nashville: Boardman & Holmes , 1998.

Rooker, Mark. *Holman Old Testament Commentary: Ezekiel.* Nashville: Broadman & Holman Publishers, 2005.

Schreiner, Thomas R. *The New American Commentary: 1, 2 Peter, Jude.* Nashville: Broadman & Holman, 2003.

Sisson, Dick. *Evangelism* XE **"Evangelism"** \b *Encounter.* Chicago, IL: Victor Books, 1988.

Stein, Robert H. *A Basic Guide to Interpreting the Bible: Playing by the Rules.* Grand Rapids: Baker Books, 1994.

Stetzer, Ed, and David Putman. *Breaking the Missional Code: Your Church Can Become a Missionary in Your Community.* Nashville: Broadman & Holman, 2006.

Stott, John. *The Art of Preaching in the Twentieth Century: Between Two Worlds.* Grand Rapids, MI: Wm. B. Eerdmans, 1994.

Sutton, Jerry. *A Primer on Biblical Preaching.* Bloomington, IN: CrossBooks, 2011.

Vine, W E. *Vine's Expository Dictionary of Old and New Testament Words.* Nashville: Thomas Nelson, 1996.

Wallace, Daniel. *Greek Grammar Beyond the Basics.* Grad Rapids: Zondervan, 1996.

Walls, David, and Max Anders. *Holman New Testament Commentary: I & II Peter, I, II & III John, Jude.* Nashville: Broadman & Holman Publishers, 1996.

Weber, Stuart K. *Holman New Testament Commentary, vol. 1, Matthew.* Nashville, TN: Broadman & Holman Publishers, 2000.

Wood, D R W. *New Bible Dictionary (Third Edition).* Downers Grove: InterVarsity Press, 1996.

Zodhiates, Spiros. *The Complete Word Study Dictionary: New Testament.* Chattanooga: AMG Publishers, 2000, c1992, c1993.

www.ingramcontent.com/pod-product-compliance
Lightning Source LLC
LaVergne TN
LVHW051350080426
835509LV00020BA/3371